Two-Hour Teddy Bears

ANITA

Two-Hour Teddy Bears

Anita Louise Crane

Sterling Publishing Co., Inc. New York
A Sterling/Chapelle Book

CHAPELLE:

- Owner: Jo Packham
- Editor: Karmen Quinney
- Staff: Marie Barber, Ann Bear, Areta Bingham, Peggy Bowers, Kass Burchett, Rebecca Christensen, Holly Fuller, Marilyn Goff, Shirley Heslop, Holly Hollingsworth, Sherry Hoppe, Shawn Hsu, Susan Jorgensen, Pauline Locke, Barbara Milburn, Linda Orton, Leslie Ridenour, Cindy Stoeckl
- Photography: Anita Louise Crane
  Kevin Dilley/Hazen Photography
- Photostylist: Anita Louise Crane
- Illustrations: Anita Louise Crane

We would like to offer our sincere appreciation for the valuable support given in this ever changing industry of new ideas, concepts, designs, and products. Several projects shown in this publication were created with the outstanding and innovative products developed by EDINBURGH IMPORTS, INC. OF NEWBURY PARK, CA; INTERCAL TRADING OF COSTA MESA, CA; PFAFF AMERICA SALES CORP. OF PARAMUS, NJ; and SPARE BEAR PARTS CATALOG OF INTERLOCKEN, MI.

Library of Congress Cataloging-in-Publication Data

Crane, Anita Louise.
Two-hour teddy bears / Anita Louise Crane.
p. cm.
"A Sterling/Chapelle Book."
Includes index.
ISBN 0-8069-3800-5
1. Soft toy making. 2. Teddy Bears I. Title.
TT174.3.C74 1998 98-26734
745.592'43–dc21 CIP

10 9 8 7 6 5 4 3 2 1

First paperback edition published in 2000 by
Sterling Publishing Company, Inc.
387 Park Avenue South, New York, N.Y. 10016

Distributed in Canada by Sterling Publishing
c/o Canadian Manda Group, One Atlantic Avenue, Suite 105
Toronto, Ontario, Canada M6K 3E7
Distributed in Great Britain and Europe by Cassell PLC
Wellington House, 125 Strand, London WC2R 0BB, England
Distributed in Australia by Capricorn Link (Australia) Pty Ltd.
P.O. Box 6651, Baulkham Hills, Business Centre, NSW 2153, Australia
Printed in China

Sterling ISBN 0-8069-3800-5 Trade
0-8069-4327-0 Paper

If you have any questions or comments or would like information on specialty products featured in this book, please contact:
Chapelle Ltd., Inc., P.O. Box 9252 Ogden, UT 84409 (801) 621-2777 • FAX (801) 621-2788

A SPECIAL THANK YOU

Thank you for buying this book. I hope you have as much enjoyment creating these adorable characters as I did. Each character started as a dream and came to life as I drafted out the patterns and stitched up the prototypes. After I was satisfied with the design, I posed him/her and painted a portrait in watercolor. I wanted each bear or bunny to appear as if they were stepping out of a storybook.

The patterns are simple and quick to sew. I have eliminated extra pieces and sewing of complicated curves. The bears have no paw pads or jointing mechanisms that require special tools and supplies. All the materials you will need should be available at your local fabric store and craft supply center. Craft magazines featuring teddy bears would also list advertisements for catalog suppliers. Tools required are most household sewing and tool box supplies. The extra long "doll" needle should be available at most craft suppliers in the doll making department. The fur required in most patterns is synthetic fur or felt and is available in most fabric stores.

I would like to thank Jossy Lownes, my watercolor teacher, for everything she has taught me about painting.

A special thanks to my husband, Bruce, for his support and appreciation of my art; and to my kitty, Raisen, for keeping my feet warm while I sew and paint.

Happy Bear Making!

DEDICATION

I would like to dedicate this book to the memory of my mother, Rose, who always took such delight in my creations.

I love you, Mom.

Table of Contents

Bear Necessities

WORK AREA

Taking a little time in the beginning for organizing a work area will make projects go more quickly. Organize projects by steps, doing all the cutting at once, all machine sewing at once, all stuffing at once, and so forth.

SAFETY

The projects in this book are for decorative purposes and not intended for children. If sewing a bear for a baby or small child, check to be certain fabrics meet safety requirements, and that eyes are safety-lock or embroidered. Buttons and ribbons are also not safe for little ones. Use the common sense that you would normally use for the safety of the children in your home.

TOOLS & MATERIALS

Tools and materials required for making these teddy bears are mostly available at craft and sewing supply centers. Check local discount marts, craft and sewing supply centers, chain craft stores, and quilt supply stores. Another possibility is upholstery shops. Check local book store magazine counters for craft magazines featuring teddy bears. These will have advertisements for mail-order suppliers that carry various tools and materials.

The following tools and materials will be very helpful in creating your teddy bear:

Tools

Awl – for punching holes eyes

Cardboard – for creating sturdy patterns and templates

Craft scissors – for cutting patterns

Doll needle (5" or longer) – for stitching all the way through head and body

Embroidery needle – for use with embroidery floss

Fabric marker – for transferring pattern markings onto fabric (Fabric markers with disappearing ink seem to work best.)

Fabric scissors – for cutting fabric

Iron/ironing board – for pressing fabrics

Kitchen funnel – for placing plastic pellets into body

Measuring tape – for measuring fabric and thread

Mustache trimmer – for trimming snouts (Battery operated will work best.)

Pencil – for tracing patterns onto tracing paper

Pins – for attaching pattern pieces together and for marking ear and eye placements. (Dressmaker's pins, with large beaded top, work best because they are more visible in fur.)

Pliers – for pulling needles and thread through thick areas

Sewing machine – for sewing fabric pieces together

Sewing needle – for use with sewing thread

Stuffing stick – for pushing stuffing into bear (Many prepackaged stuffing materials contain a stuffing stick.)

Tracing paper – for tracing patterns

Transparent tape – for taping pattern pieces together

Materials

Embroidery floss – for attaching arms and legs onto body and stitching nose and mouth

Fabric – for clothing (Prewashed 100% cotton is preferred for a softer look and feel. Old wool skirts, sweaters, and blankets are also wonderful

Different types of fur: (top row) 1/2" mohair, short mohair, sparse mohair, alpaca low-nap wool; (bottom row) felt, low-loft quilt batting, synthetic long-nap fur, fuzzy felt

fabrics. It is always fun and a good idea to recycle old items. Especially if an old blanket or shirt has some sentiment. See "Bearheart" on page 42.)

Felt – for body and nose (It does not fray or need to be hemmed or lined.)

Fuzzy felt – for body (It looks very much like plush fur. It is inexpensive and wonderful to work with when creating a bear or bunny.)

Glass eyes – for eyes (They have a wire loop for attaching. These are only for adult collectors, and are not considered safe for small children.)

Heavy thread – for attaching head, arms, and legs to body (Carpet, upholstery, and quilting are heavy threads that work well.)

Low-loft quilt batting – for body (It can be dyed with coffee or tea if a darker color is desired.)

Mohair – for body (It is a wonderful fabric for creating a traditional bear. However, it is expensive because it is imported from Germany or England.)

Plastic pellets – for weighing bears down so they can sit or stand on their own

Plastic pellets for stuffing

Polyester stuffing – for stuffing (It is safe and allergy proof. It is also available in a heavier-weight stuffing called hard pack.)

Safety eyes – for eyes (They have a locking disc that holds them in place, and are considered safe for children.)

Sewing thread – for tacking clothing on bears

Synthetic fur – for body (It has a tendency to stretch, which works well for sculpting and molding faces.)

Pattern pieces that have been cut and pinned with matching pieces

PATTERNS

1. Using pencil, trace patterns onto tracing paper.

2. Using craft scissors, cut out patterns and trace pattern onto cardboard for template. Using fabric marker, transfer all markings, such as openings, eye, and ear placement, and fold, onto fabric.

3. Using craft scissors, cut out cardboard template pieces. When laying out template pieces on fur, follow direction of nap. To determine nap direction, simply smooth your hand across fur to see which way fur lays.

CUTTING

1. Lay out pattern pieces on back of fur or felt fabric, checking carefully for nap directions. Using fabric marker, trace pattern onto fabric. It helps to mark an arrow on back of fur in direction of nap.

2. Using tips of fabric scissors, make little snips, cutting backing of fur only.

3. Match pattern pieces, such as ears, arms, legs, and body pieces.

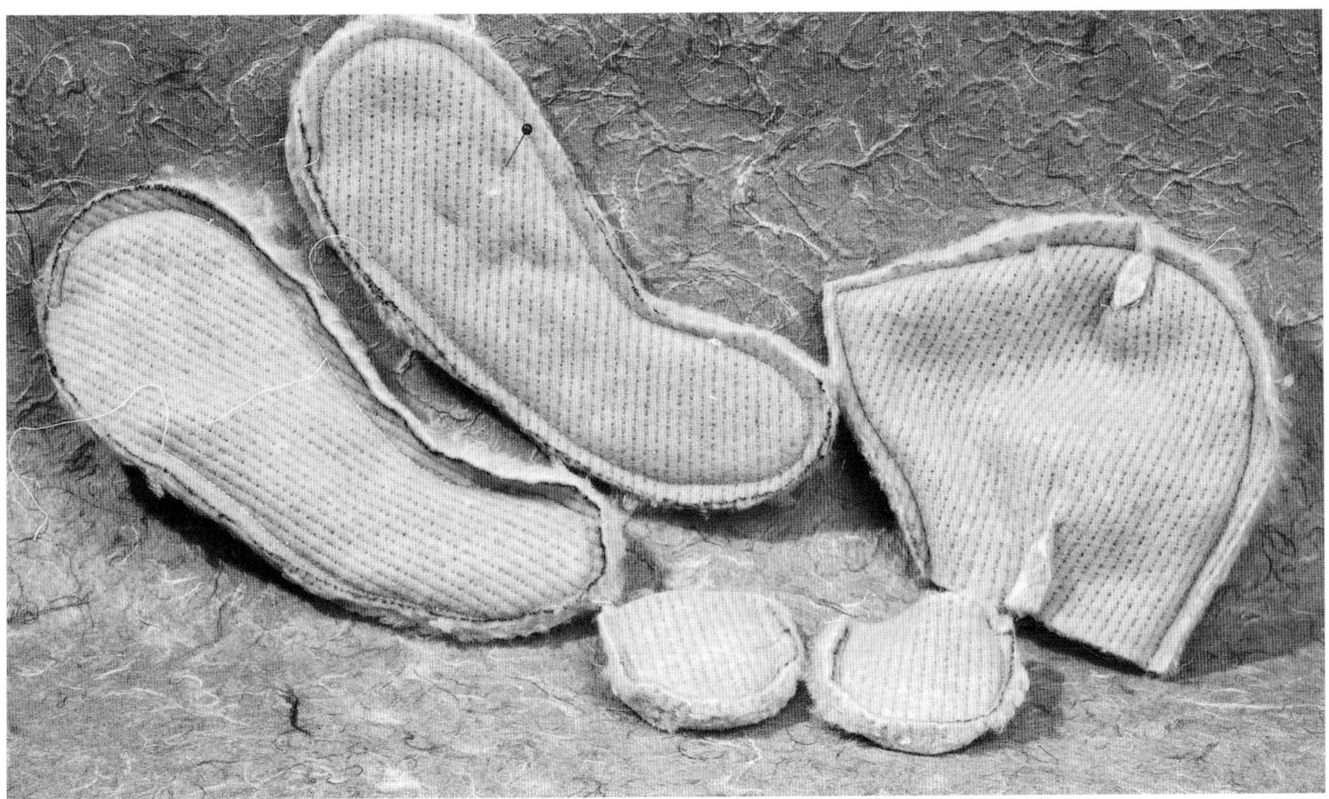

Pattern pieces after being sewn

SEWING

A $^{1}/_{8}$" seam allowance has been included in all patterns in this book. Although marking the seam allowance on fabric helps in visualizing stitches that are going to be made, most sewing machines have indicators to help you follow an exact seam allowance. Sew all darts first. Use a small stitch on your machine so that going around curves is much easier. Setting your needle to stop down in the fabric also makes turning pieces simpler.

Head

1. Using pins, pin two head pieces, with right sides together.

2. Using sewing machine, sew from nose to bottom of neck. Sew from nose around head to bottom edge, leaving open at bottom. Trim close but not too close to seam at nose area.

3. Remove pins. Turn right side out.

Ears

1. Using pins, pin opposite pieces with right sides together.

2. Using sewing machine, sew around ears, leaving open at bottom.

3. Remove pins. Turn right side out.

Body

Note: Most projects use the following steps for sewing bear's body. For bears with four body pieces follow individual project instructions.

1. Using pins, pin left and right back pieces together, where applicable.

2. Using sewing machine, sew from top to bottom, leaving open where indicated on pattern.

3. Pin left and right pieces together where applicable. Sew from top to bottom of front.

4. Pin front section to back section with right sides facing, matching side seams. Starting at top, sew all the way around.

5. Remove pins. Turn right side out.

Arms & Legs

1. Using pins, pin outside arm piece to inside arm piece, with right sides facing.

2. Using sewing machine, sew pieces together all the way around, leaving open where indicated on pattern.

3. Remove pins. Turn right side out. Repeat for other arm.

4. Using pins, pin outside leg piece to inside leg piece, with right sides facing.

5. Using sewing machine, sew pieces together all the way around, leaving open where indicated on pattern.

6. Remove pins. Turn right side out. Repeat for other leg.

STUFFING

A sewn section that is ready to be stuffed with plastic pellets and polyester stuffing

1. Stuff all sewn sections, except body and ears. (If using safety eyes, mark and insert eyes before stuffing. After inserting eyes, stuff and proceed with nose template and ears.) The body in most projects has plastic pellets inserted first, then top is filled with polyester stuffing. (A kitchen funnel can be used to fill body with pellets.)

2. Using stuffing stick, methodically stuff head from top opening with little pieces of polyester stuffing. Stuff nose firmly. Sculpt head by shaping as you stuff.

3. Using embroidery needle, plump up cheeks and bottom of nose.

4. See "Ladder Stitch" on page 15. When stuffing is complete, sew all sections closed with Ladder Stitch.

Sewn sections after being stuffed

Stuffing Tips:

For all sections of the bear, stuff hard-to-reach parts first.

For a soft bear, stuff paw and feet hard and then lighten up as you move up limb.

For emergency repairs, stuff fur scraps in body of bear so that fur will be available.

For an even-looking bear, stuff all parts firmly and evenly.

For a huggable bear, test firmness of each section before sewing that section closed.

Bear head in tea cup for placement marking

DESIGNING THE FACE

Pattern pieces have markings for location of eyes and ears. However, you can experiment for the look you prefer.

1. Try moving pins around, using larger or smaller nose and even using a larger and smaller eye.

2. Choose desired eye color.

3. Have fun personalizing your creation. Safety eyes are inserted before stuffing. Glass eyes are attached after head is completely stuffed.

Placement

1. After stuffing head, place head in tea cup to hold upright.

2. Using pins, mark eye placement.

3. See "Satin Stitch" on page 15. Pin nose template onto face. Using embroidery needle, embroider nose over template with embroidery floss and Satin Stitch. Embroider mouth.

4. Using pins, pin ears in place. Remove ears, leaving pins to mark where ears are to be sewn, after eyes have been completed.

Glass Eyes

1. Using fabric scissors, cut 12" length of heavy thread. Thread through eye loop, then thread doll needle with both tails of thread. Crimp loop flat with pliers.

2. Insert needle into eye placement marked with pin, going all the way through head with needle and out back seam near neck. Repeat for other side coming out on opposite seam $^1/_2$" from other threads.

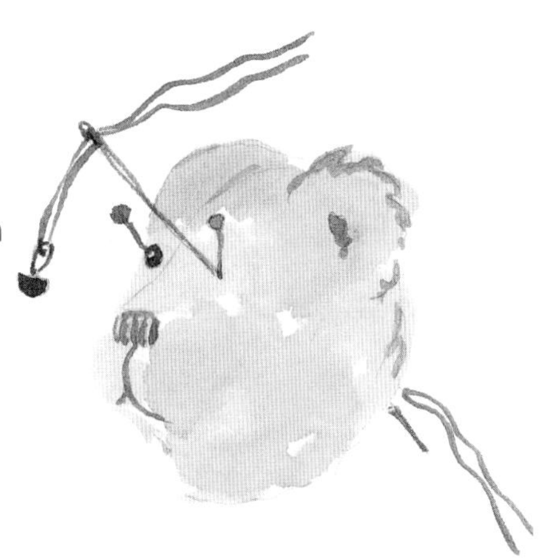

3. Pull threads tightly to indent eyes into fur and tie into double knot. Rethread doll needle with all tails of threads and pull into head. Trim.

Safety Eyes

1. Using fabric marker, mark placement for eyes.

2. Using an awl, make small hole on mark. Push safety eye through and from inside of head, press safety lock onto eye shank. Press very tightly until lock disc goes all the way down.

3. Repeat for other eye. Now head is ready to stuff.

Nose & Mouth

1. Using pencil, transfer desired nose pattern onto tracing paper. Using fabric marker, trace desired nose and mouth pattern from patterns on this page onto felt.

2. Using fabric scissors, cut pattern from felt, creating template. Using pins, pin felt nose onto face.

3. See "Satin Stitch" on facing page. Using embroidery needle, embroider over felt nose with embroidery floss and Satin Stitch. Keep tension even and tight and untwist threads as you go. Follow illustration for mouth.

4. If you are not satisfied with the appearance, snip embroidered pieces and pull out thread, using pliers. Keep cutting and restitching until you like appearance of nose and mouth.

Nose & Mouth Patterns

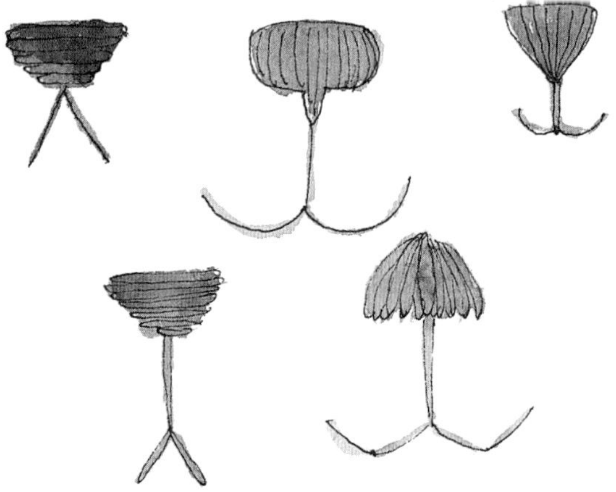

A bear's nose while being embroidered

ATTACHING STUFFED SECTIONS

Ears to Head

1. See "Ladder Stitch" on bottom right. Using embroidery needle, sew ear to head with heavy thread and Ladder Stitch, where marked, curving ears as you stitch.

2. Knot thread and pull ends of thread into head. Cut off excess thread. Repeat for other ear.

Arms & Legs to Body

1. Using doll needle with heavy thread, doubled about 3' long, take needle through arm, through body where indicated on pattern for arm position, and through second arm. (Pliers can help pull thread through thick areas.)

2. Thread on a button, then take needle back through arm, body, and first arm.

3. Thread on another button with needle and thread ending up between button and arm. Pull threads tightly. Wrap thread around button and knot. Pull ends of thread into body. Repeat for legs. See photo on page 16.

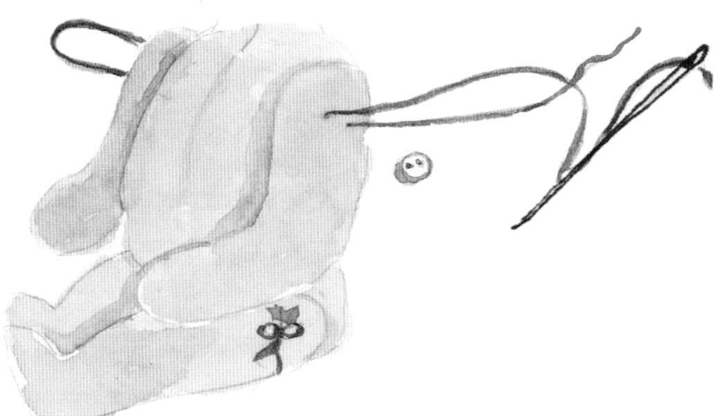

Head to Body

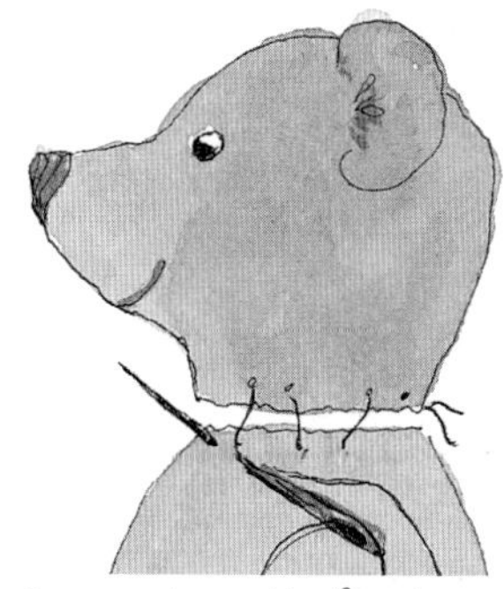

1. See "Ladder Stitch" below. Using embroidery needle, sew head to body with heavy thread and Ladder Stitch, lining up center of head and body.

2. Sew around neck twice to insure head is firmly attached.

3. Pull knot and ends of thread into body.

STITCHES

Blanket Stitch

1. Bring needle up at A; go down at B. Bring needle up again at C, keeping thread under needle. Go down at D and repeat.

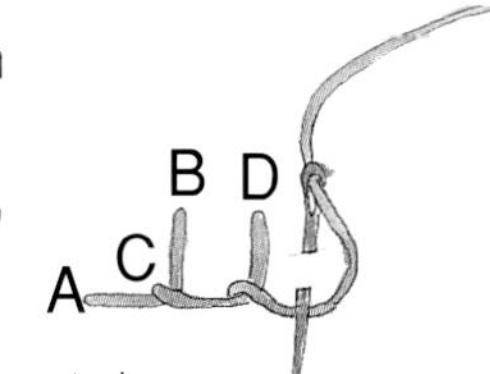

2. Make all stitches equal in size and shape.

Ladder Stitch

1. Knot thread. Go in first edge at A and out 1/4" at B. Drop down to next joining edge and out at C. Go in 1/4" at D, and back up to other edge at E.

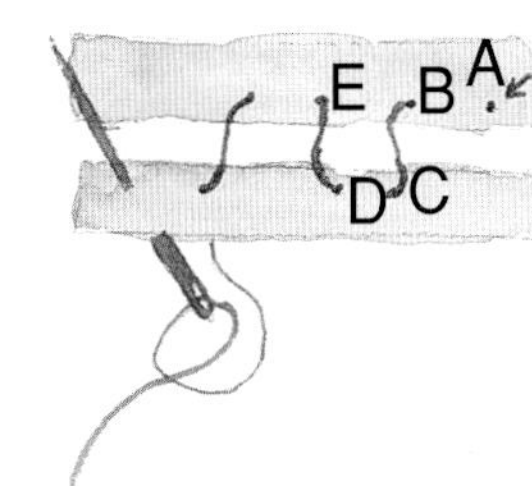

2. Repeat and pull tightly as needed.

Satin Stitch

1. Keep thread smooth and flat. Bring needle up at A; go down at B, forming a straight stitch. Bring needle up again at C. Go down at D, forming another straight stitch next to the first.

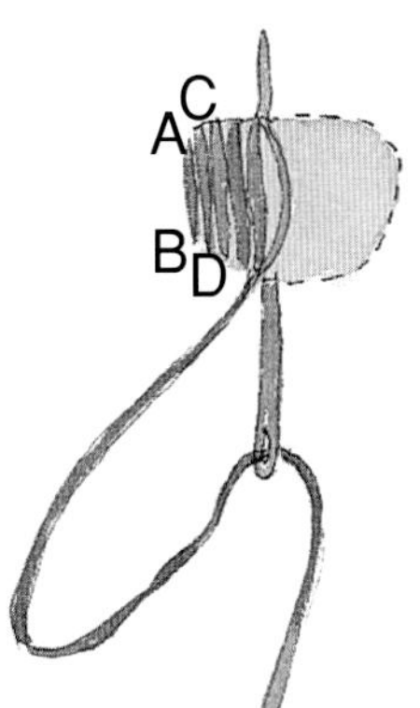

2. Repeat to fill design area.

Bear after attaching sections (Notice the buttons that join the arms and legs to the body.)

GLUING

If a sewing machine is not available for creating a project, try gluing pattern pieces together with fabric glue. Fabric glue is not recommend when using expensive mohair. Most seams can be glued. However, seams such as darts and closures are best done by stitching. Attaching the head is also best done by stitching. Fabric glue is not recommended for bears that will be given to children.

Most of the projects in this book can be glued. However, the following patterns will give the best results when assembled with fabric glue: Miss Willow, Miss Parsley, Rachael, Helouise, Santa Bear, and Amy Rabbit. The other patterns have a number of smaller pieces with more complicated curves that make them harder to glue.

1. Read instructions and precautions on back of fabric glue bottle.

2. Using mustache trimmer, trim fuzzy furs to 1/8" at edges to provide a nice clean edge to which fabric glue can adhere.

3. Using fabric glue, squeeze thin line along fabric edge 2" at a time. Working quickly and methodically, press edges together and proceed until all seams are completed.

4. Allow fabric glue to dry for at least 10 minutes before turning sections right side out.

Gluing Tips:

Use in well ventilated areas.

Keep away from flame.

Protect work surface with newspaper.

Practice folding and gluing on scraps of chosen fabric before gluing actual project.

Use a paper towel to protect hands from excess glue that seeps out of seam.

Renditions: Please note that artist's bear portraits, illustrations, and drawings are not drawn to project specification.

Miss Parsley and Miss Willow, chatting over tea

Miss Willow is similar to Helouise, who is on page 37, except she is much larger and has a very fat face. She also carries a basket that you can fill with sewing supplies, baked bread, or fruit. You might even try some flowers or twigs for firewood. She has a nice skirt and shawl, and sometimes she wears a straw hat. Her body is made from cotton flannel and her head and arms from synthetic fur. Find a fur with a low nap—a plush or sparse fur.

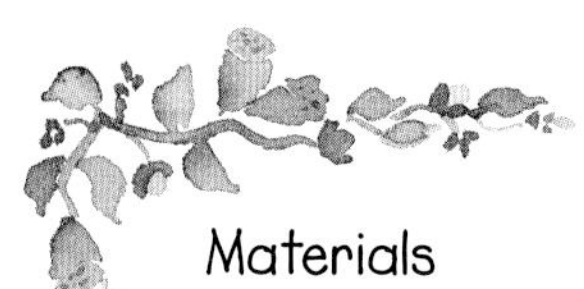

Materials

Buttons: medium (2); small
Embroidery floss: brown
Eyelet lace: 8"-wide (10")
Eyes: glass or safety, 8 mm, black
Fabrics: felt square (scrap) for nose; flannel (1/2 yd.) for body and skirt; synthetic fur (1/4 yd.) for arms, ears, and head; wool (1/4 yd.) for shawl
Plastic pellets: (1 cup)
Polyester stuffing: small bag
Ribbon: coordinating color of choice, width of choice (1 yd.)
Straw basket: small
Thread: heavy; sewing, coordinating color of choice

Tools

Cardboard
Fabric marker
Measuring tape
Needles: doll, 5" or longer; embroidery; sewing
Pencil
Pins
Scissors: craft; fabric
Sewing machine with thread
Stuffing stick
Tracing paper
Transparent tape

All seam allowances are 1/8".

Beginnings

1. Read "Bear Necessities" on pages 8–17 before beginning. Organize all materials and tools needed for this project.

2. Using pencil, tracing paper, cardboard, and craft scissors, make templates of pattern pieces on pages 21–23.

3. Place templates on backs of fabric. Using fabric marker, trace pattern. Using fabric scissors, cut out fabric pieces.

4. Using sewing machine, sew darts in head.

5. Sew head, ear, and arm pieces, with right sides together, leaving open where marked.

6. Sew body pieces, with right sides together, leaving open where marked. Square off bottom corners by folding bottom seam flat and sewing across corners. Check all seams. Turn all sewn pieces right side out.

Note: If using glass eyes, stuff head first. If using safety eyes, insert eyes first and then stuff head.

7. Using stuffing stick, stuff head firmly with polyester stuffing. Stuff arms. Fill bottom of body with plastic pellets, then stuff body firmly to the top with polyester stuffing.

Face

8. Using pins, mark eye placement. Using doll needle, pull eyes onto face with heavy thread.

9. Using pins, attach ears onto head where marked on pattern. See "Ladder Stitch" on page 15. Using embroidery needle, sew ears onto head with heavy thread and Ladder Stitch.

10. Using pencil, trace desired nose pattern from page 14 onto tracing paper, creating template. Using craft scissors, cut out template. Using fabric marker, trace template onto felt. Using fabric scissors, cut out felt nose. Pin felt nose onto face.

11. See "Satin Stitch" on page 15. Using embroidery needle, embroider over felt nose with embroidery floss and Satin Stitch. Embroider mouth.

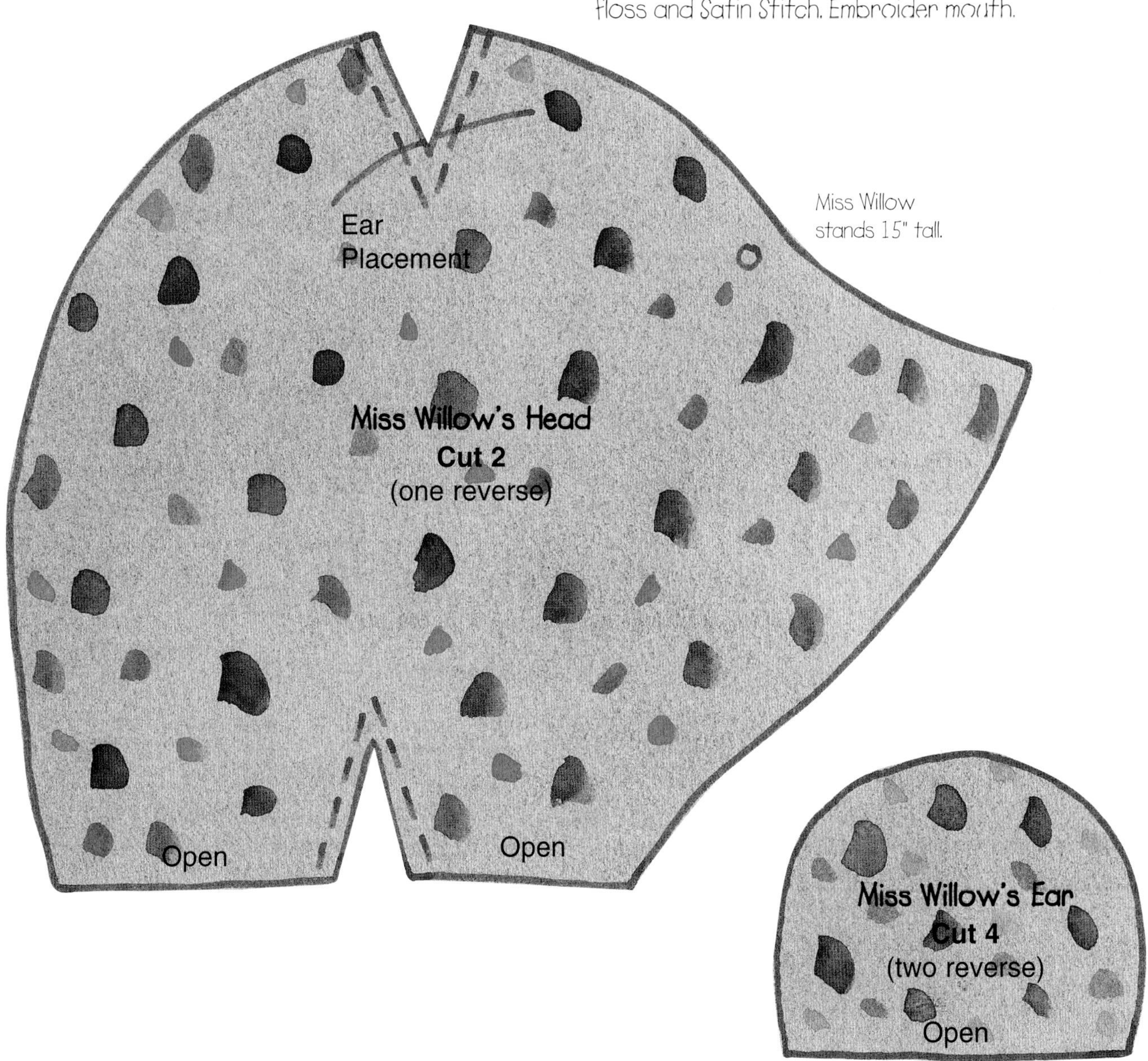

Miss Willow stands 15" tall.

Arms & Body

12. Using embroidery needle, gather-stitch around opening on body with heavy thread, leaving slightly open to fit base of head. Sew arms closed.

13. Using doll needle, sew arms onto body with heavy thread and buttons.

14. Align center of head and body. See "Ladder Stitch" on page 15. Using embroidery needle, sew head onto body with heavy thread and Ladder Stitch. Sew around neck twice for strength.

♥ See completed bear on page 24 before adding clothing.

Skirt

15. Using fabric scissors, cut 10" x 24" piece of flannel fabric for skirt.

16. Using measuring tape, measure waist of bear. Using fabric scissors, cut 2"-wide band the length of waist measurement from flannel fabric, creating waistband.

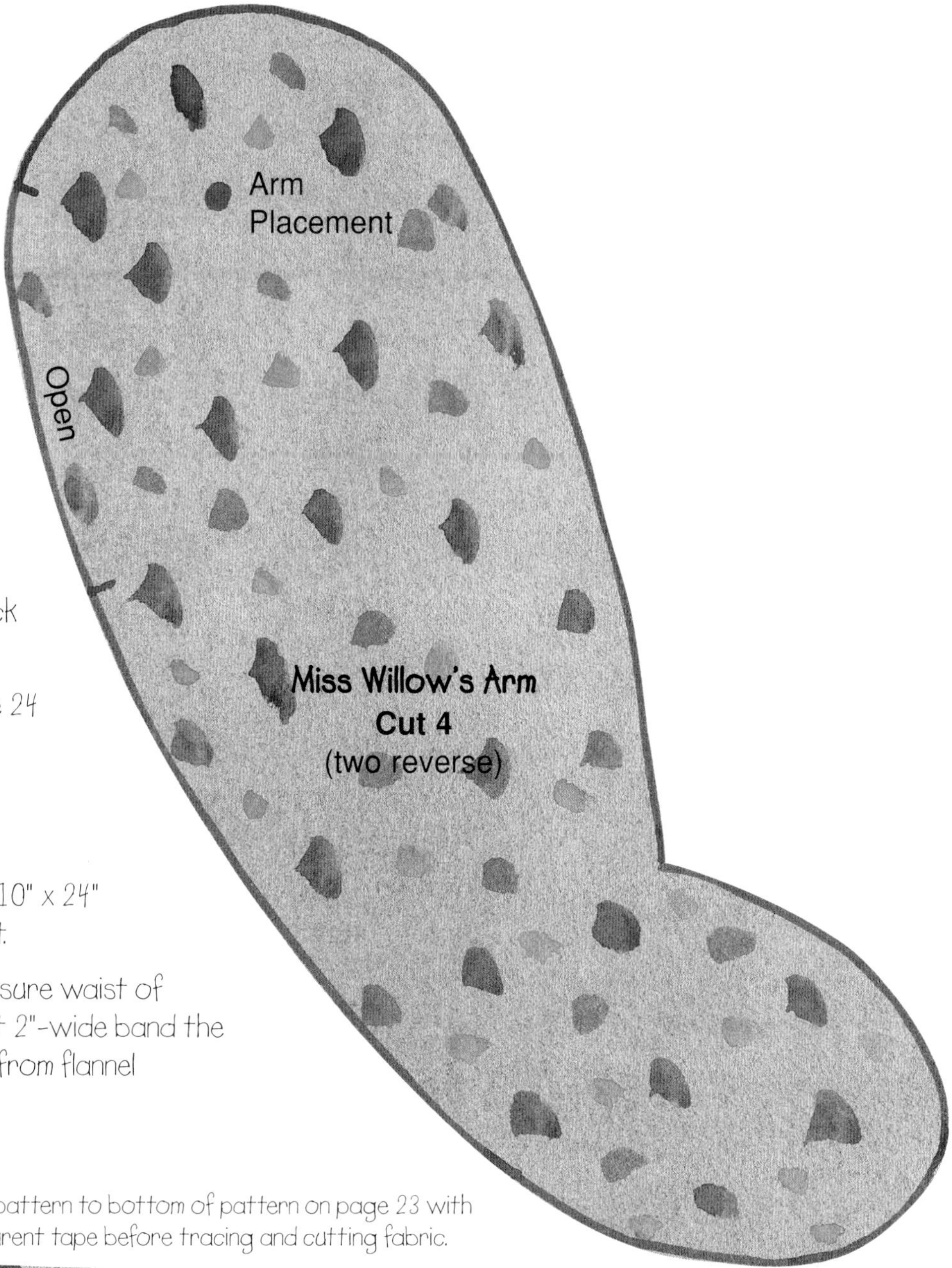

Arm Placement

Open

Miss Willow's Arm
Cut 4
(two reverse)

Attach pattern to bottom of pattern on page 23 with transparent tape before tracing and cutting fabric.

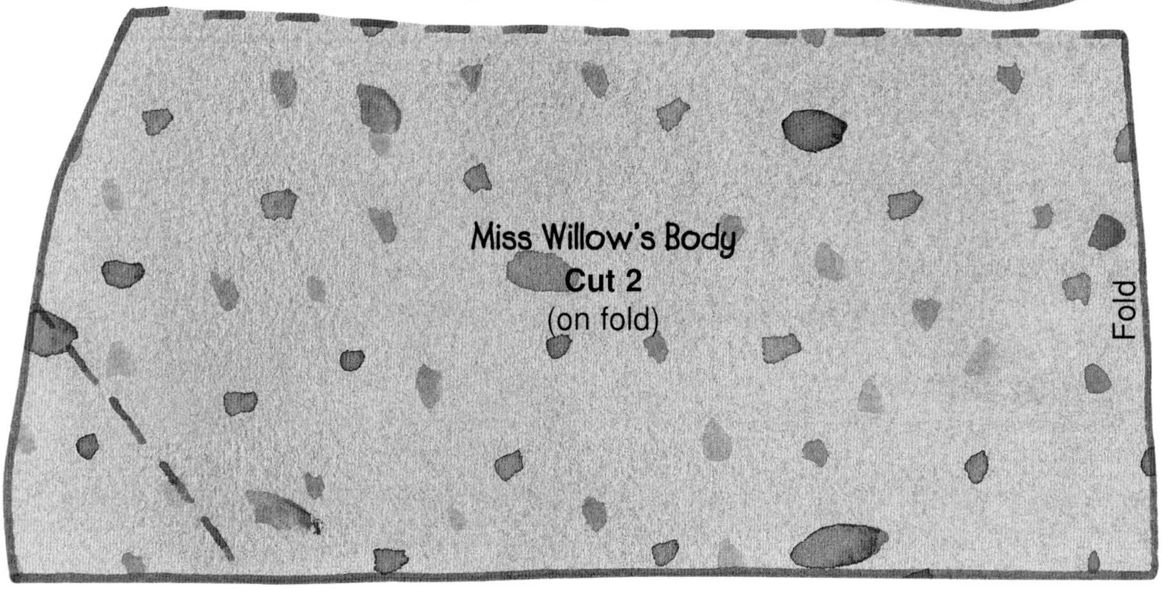

Miss Willow's Body
Cut 2
(on fold)

Fold

17. Using sewing machine, gather-stitch top long edge of skirt and sew onto waistband. Sew side seam. Turn waistband down and stitch on inside. Hem skirt to desired length.

18. Place skirt on bear.

Apron

19. Using fabric scissors, cut 8" x 10" piece of eyelet lace.

20. Using sewing machine, gather-stitch top long edge of eyelet lace. Center ribbon on top of gather and sew, leaving ends free on sides for apron ties. Tie apron around bear's waist.

Shawl

21. Using fabric scissors, cut 8" x 18" piece of wool fabric for shawl.

22. Using sewing needle, pull threads out along all edges to create fringe.

23. Wrap shawl around shoulders. Using sewing needle, tack to secure with sewing thread. See photo on page 19 for button placement. Sew small button on shawl.

Finishings

24. Place straw basket on arm. Sew paws together.

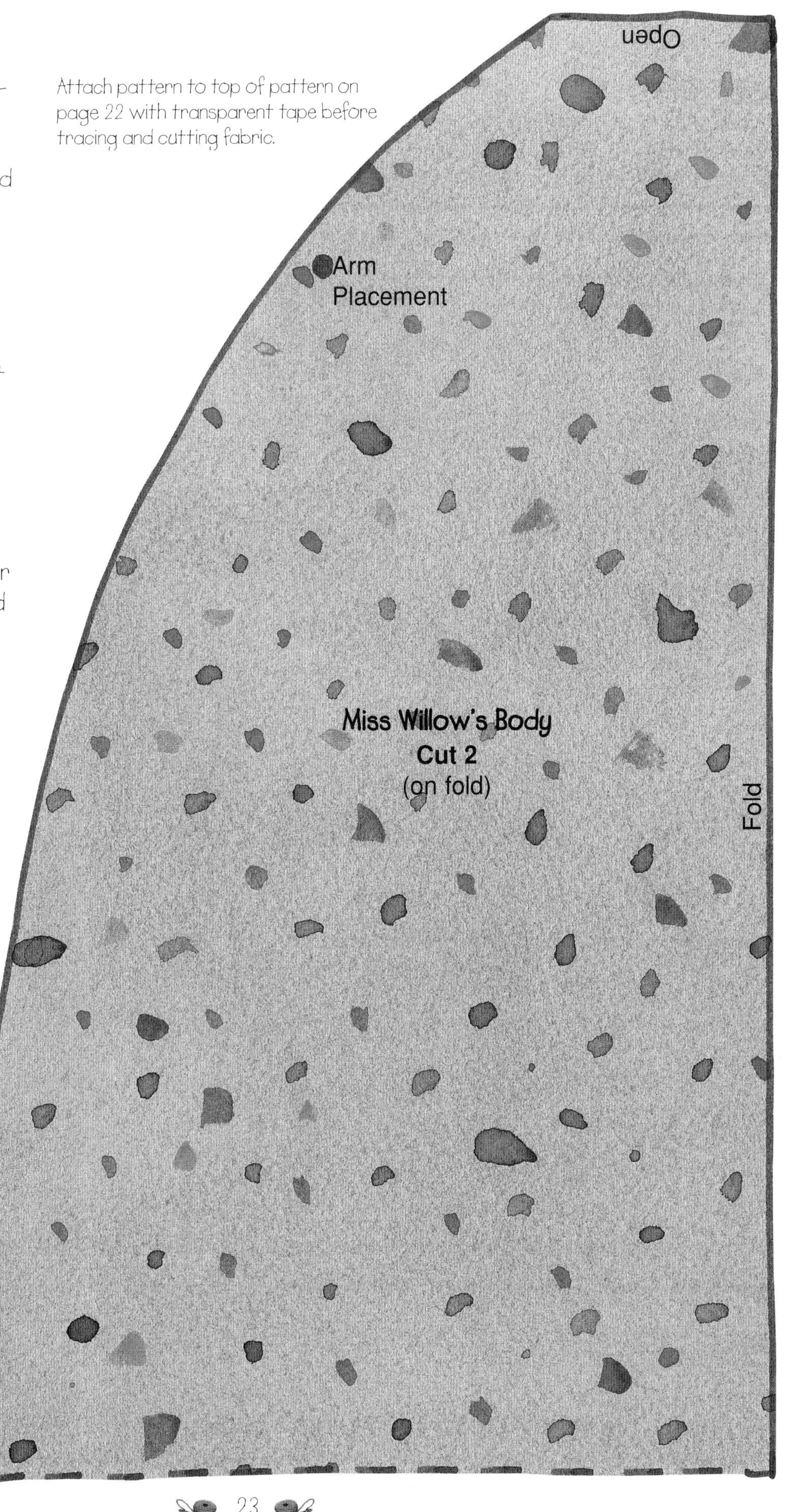

Miss Willow before adding clothing

Miss Parsley is sewn just like teddy bear, Miss Willow, who is on page 19, except she has a rounder nose and longer ears. You can sew her ears pointing up or down. Her whiskers are heavy thread pulled through the nose area with a knot in the middle to hold thread in place.

Materials

Buttons: medium (2)
Decorative pin: small
Embroidery floss: brown or pink
Eyes: glass or safety, 10 mm, black with topaz
Fabrics: cotton, white (1/4 yd.) for apron; felt, mohair, or synthetic fur (1/4 yd.) for arms, ears, and head; felt square (scrap) for nose; flannel (1/2 yd.) for body and skirt; wool (1/4 yd.) for shawl
Lace trim: 5/8"-wide (10"); (scrap)
Plastic fruit or vegetable: small
Plastic pellets: (1 cup)
Polyester stuffing: small bag
Ribbon: coordinating color of choice, 1"-wide (1 yd.)
Thread: heavy; sewing, coordinating color of choice

Tools

Cardboard
Fabric marker
Measuring tape
Needles: doll, 5" or longer; embroidery; sewing
Pencil
Pins
Scissors: craft; fabric
Sewing machine with thread
Stuffing stick
Tracing paper

All seam allowances are 1/8". Miss Parsley and Miss Willow share pattern pieces.

Beginnings

1. Read "Bear Necessities" on pages 8-17 before beginning. Organize all materials and tools needed for this project.

2. Using pencil, tracing paper, cardboard, and craft scissors, make templates of pattern pieces on pages 22-23 (do not trace arm) and 27-28.

3. Place templates on backs of fabric. Using fabric marker, trace pattern. Using fabric scissors, cut out fabric pieces.

4. Using sewing machine, sew darts in head.

5. Sew head, ear, and arm pieces, with right sides together, leaving open where marked.

6. Sew body pieces, with right sides together, leaving open where marked. Square off bottom corners by folding bottom seam flat and sewing across corners. Check all seams. Turn all sewn pieces right side out.

Note: If using glass eyes, stuff head first. If using safety eyes, insert eyes first and then stuff head.

7. Using stuffing stick, stuff head firmly with polyester stuffing. Stuff arms. Fill bottom of body with plastic pellets, then stuff body firmly to the top with polyester stuffing.

Miss Parsley stands 15" tall.

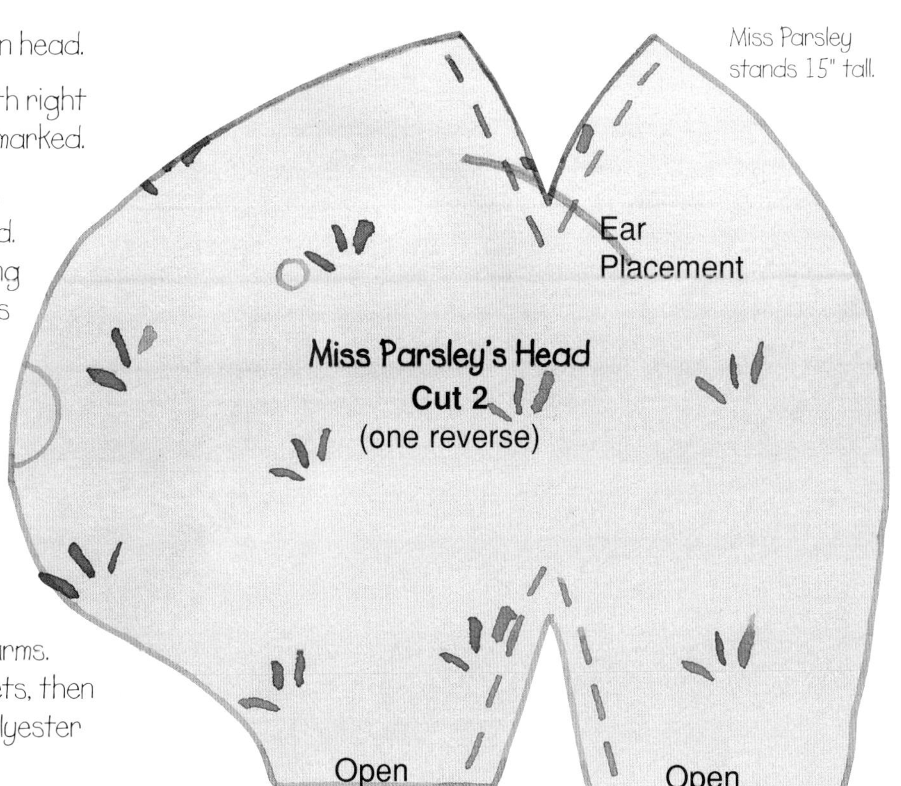

Face

8. Using pins, mark eye placement. Using doll needle, pull eyes onto face with heavy thread.

9. Using pins, attach ears onto head where marked on pattern. See "Ladder Stitch" on page 15. Using embroidery needle, sew ears onto head with heavy thread and Ladder Stitch.

10. Using pencil, trace desired nose pattern from page 14 onto tracing paper, creating template. Using craft scissors, cut out template. Using fabric marker, trace template onto felt. Using fabric scissors, cut out felt nose. Pin felt nose onto face.

11. See "Satin Stitch" on page 15. Using embroidery needle, embroider over felt nose with embroidery floss and Satin Stitch. Embroider mouth.

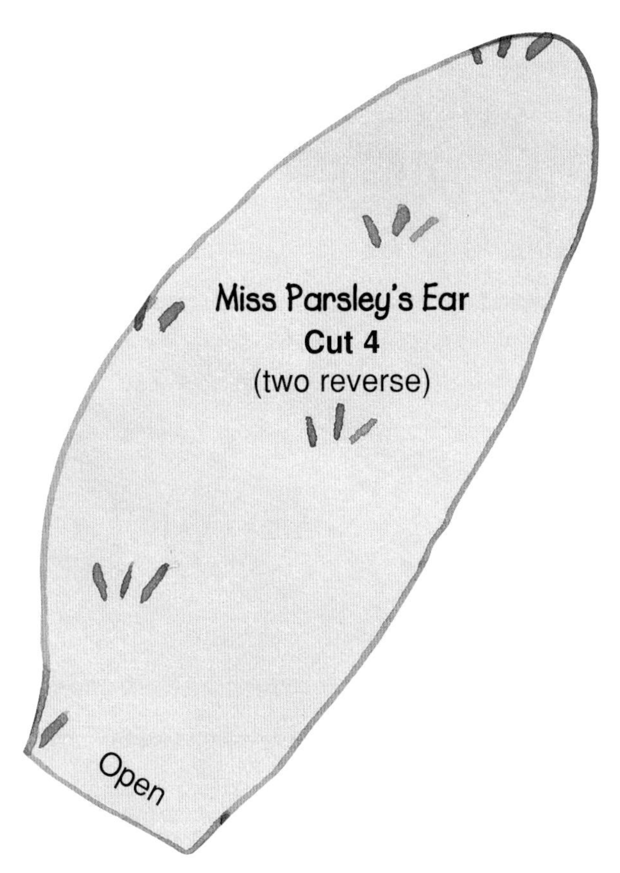

Whiskers

12. Using fabric scissors, cut 6" piece of heavy thread. Thread onto embroidery needle and tie knot in center of thread length. Pull thread into nose and yank, leaving knot inside. Repeat this step, creating four whiskers on each side of face. Using fabric scissors, trim threads.

Arms & Body

13. Using embroidery needle, gather-stitch around opening on body with heavy thread, leaving slightly open to fit base of head. Sew arms closed.

14. Using doll needle, sew arms onto body with heavy thread and buttons.

15. Align center seams of head and body. See "Ladder Stitch" on page 15. Using embroidery needle, sew head onto body with heavy thread and Ladder Stitch. Sew around neck twice for strength.

Skirt

16. Using fabric scissors, cut 10" x 24" piece of flannel fabric for skirt.

17. Using measuring tape, measure waist of bunny. Using fabric scissors, cut 2"-wide band the length of waist measurement from flannel fabric, creating waistband.

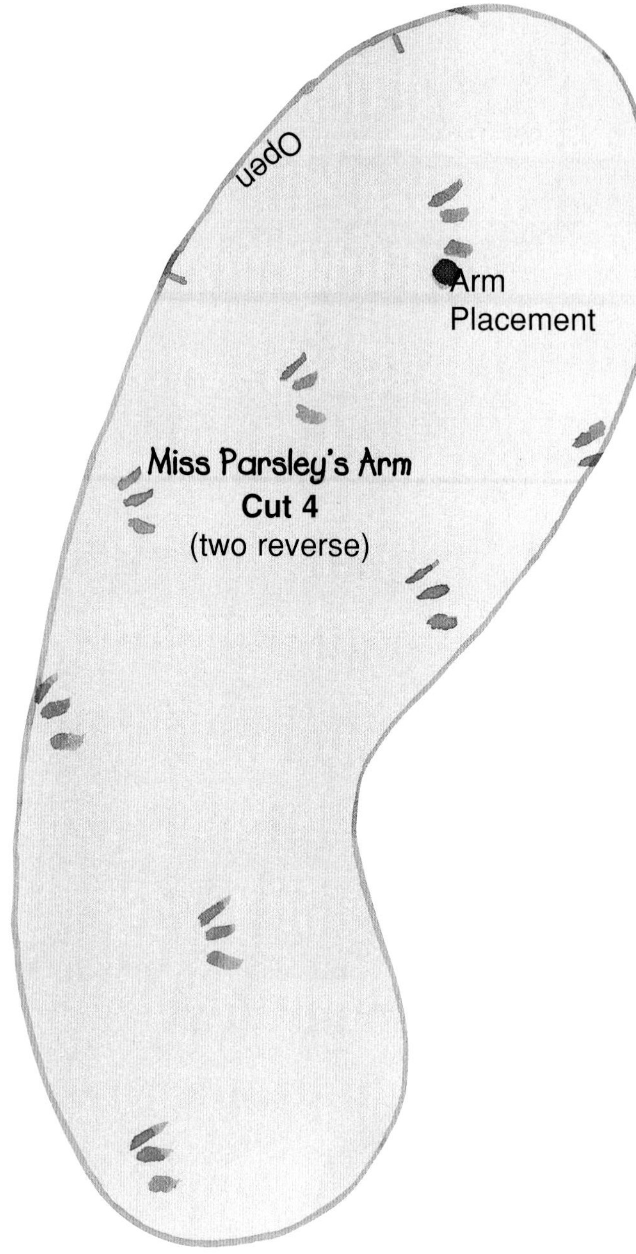

The Crumbs from our cake could be a mouse family's dinner.

18. Using sewing machine, gather-stitch top long edge of skirt and sew onto waistband. Sew side seam. Turn waistband down and stitch on inside. Hem skirt to desired length.

19. Place skirt on bunny.

Apron

20. Using fabric scissors, cut 8" x 10" piece of white fabric.

21. Using sewing machine, sew lace trim onto bottom long edge of white fabric. Turn sides in and stitch to finish edge.

22. Gather-stitch top long edge of white fabric. Center ribbon on top of gather and sew, leaving ends free on sides for apron ties. Tie apron around bunny's waist.

Shawl

23. Using fabric scissors, cut 8" x 18" piece of wool fabric.

24. Using sewing needle, pull threads out along all edges to create fringe.

25. Wrap shawl around shoulders. Using sewing needle, tack to secure with sewing thread. See photo on page 25 for decorative pin placement. Sew decorative pin on shawl.

Finishings

26. Sew paws together and place desired fruit or vegetable in arms.

Miss Parsley and friend, chatting over tea (Instructions for Miss Parsley's friend, see page 63. Reduce patterns as desired.)

Rachael has a fur head and arms. Her body is flannel. She has pellets in her body so she can stand on her own. Her shawl and apron are fashioned from antique lace. My little angels are pictured on pages 30-31, holding animals; but imagine them holding a stuffed heart or bouquet of flowers. Rachael is pictured on the left on page 30.

Materials

Bird or flowers: small
Buttons: medium (4)
Embroidery floss: brown
Eyes: glass or safety, 8 mm, black
Fabrics: felt, muslin, or print, 12" square for wings; felt square (scrap) for nose; flannel, printed (1/4 yd.) for body; felt, synthetic fur, or wool (1/4 yd.) for arms, ears, and head
Lace: collar; (scrap)
Plastic pellets: (1 cup)
Polyester stuffing: small bag
Ribbon: coordinating color of choice, width of choice (1 yd.)
Thread: heavy; sewing, coordinating color of choice

Tools

Cardboard
Fabric marker
Measuring tape
Needles: doll, 5" or longer; embroidery; sewing
Pencil
Pins
Scissors: craft; fabric
Sewing machine with thread
Stuffing stick
Tracing paper

All seam allowances are 1/8".

Beginnings

1. Read "Bear Necessities" on pages 8-17 before beginning. Organize all materials and tools needed for this project.

2. Using pencil, tracing paper, cardboard, and craft scissors, make templates of pattern pieces on pages 33-35.

3. Place templates on backs of fabric. Using fabric marker, trace pattern. Using fabric scissors, cut out fabric pieces.

4. Using sewing machine, sew head, ear, arm, and wing pieces, with right sides together, leaving open where marked.

5. Sew body pieces, with right sides together, leaving open where marked. Square off bottom corners by folding bottom seam flat and sewing across corners. Check all seams. Turn all sewn pieces right side out.

Note: If using glass eyes, stuff head first. If using safety eyes, insert eyes first and then stuff head.

6. Using stuffing stick, stuff head firmly with polyester stuffing. Stuff arms and wings. Fill bottom of body with plastic pellets, then stuff body firmly to the top with polyester stuffing.

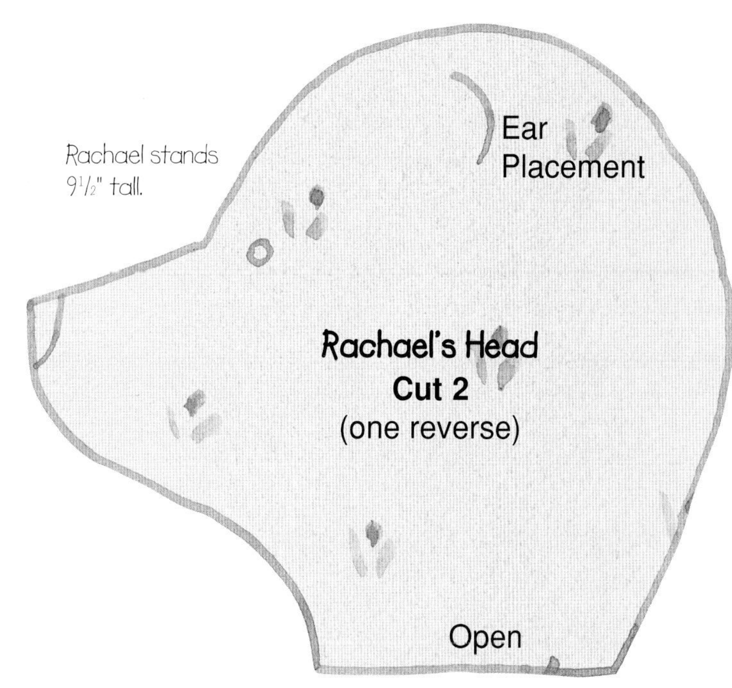

Rachael stands 9½" tall.

Face

7. Using pins, mark eye placement. Using doll needle, pull eyes onto face with heavy thread.

8. Using pins, attach ears onto head where marked on pattern. See "Ladder Stitch" on page 15. Using embroidery needle, sew ears onto head with heavy thread and Ladder Stitch.

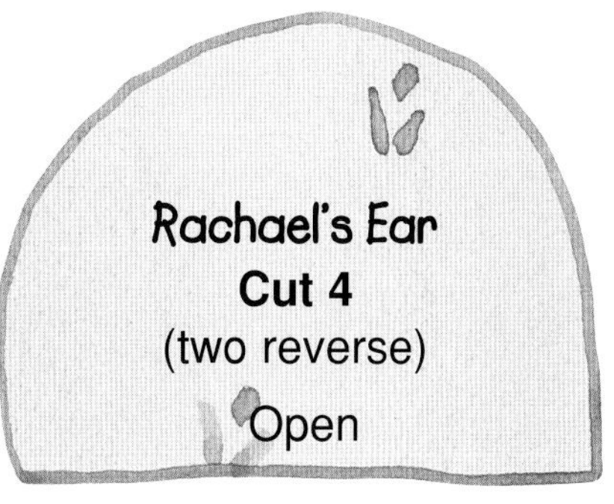

9. Using pencil, trace desired nose pattern from page 14 onto tracing paper, creating template. Using craft scissors, cut out template. Using fabric marker, trace template onto felt. Using fabric scissors, cut out nose piece. Pin felt nose onto face.

10. See "Satin Stitch" on page 15. Using embroidery needle, embroider over felt nose with embroidery floss and Satin Stitch. Embroider mouth.

To keep fabric scissors sharp, use only for fabrics.

Arms & Body

11. Using embroidery needle, gather-stitch around opening on body with heavy thread, leaving slightly open to fit base of head. Sew arms closed.

12. Using doll needle, sew arms onto body with heavy thread and buttons.

13. Align center seams of head and body. See "Ladder Stitch" on page 15. Using embroidery needle, sew head onto body with heavy thread and Ladder Stitch. Sew around neck twice for strength.

Wings

14. See pattern below. Dotted lines indicate quilting. Using sewing machine, quilt wings. Sew wings closed.

15. Using embroidery needle, sew wings onto back of bear with embroidery floss.

♥ See photo of Helouise on page 40 to view bear's form before adding clothing.

Apron

16. Place lace scrap around bear's waist. Using sewing needle, tack to secure with sewing thread.

Shawl

17. Wrap lace collar around shoulders for shawl. Tack to secure with sewing thread.

Finishings

18. Sew paws together and place a small bird or flowers in bear's arms.

19. Attach ribbon around head and waist, if desired.

Arm Placement

Open

Rachael's Arm
Cut 4
(two reverse)

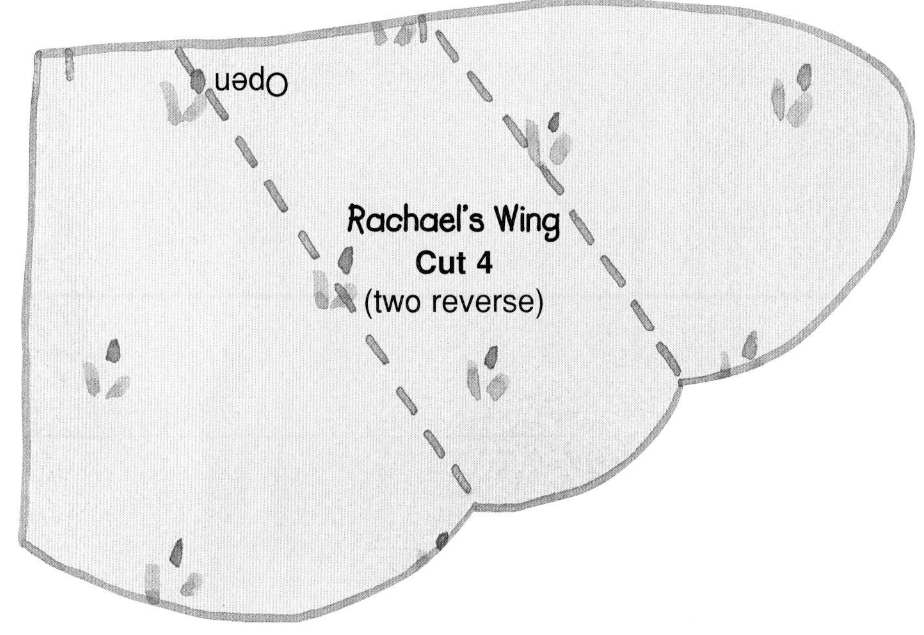

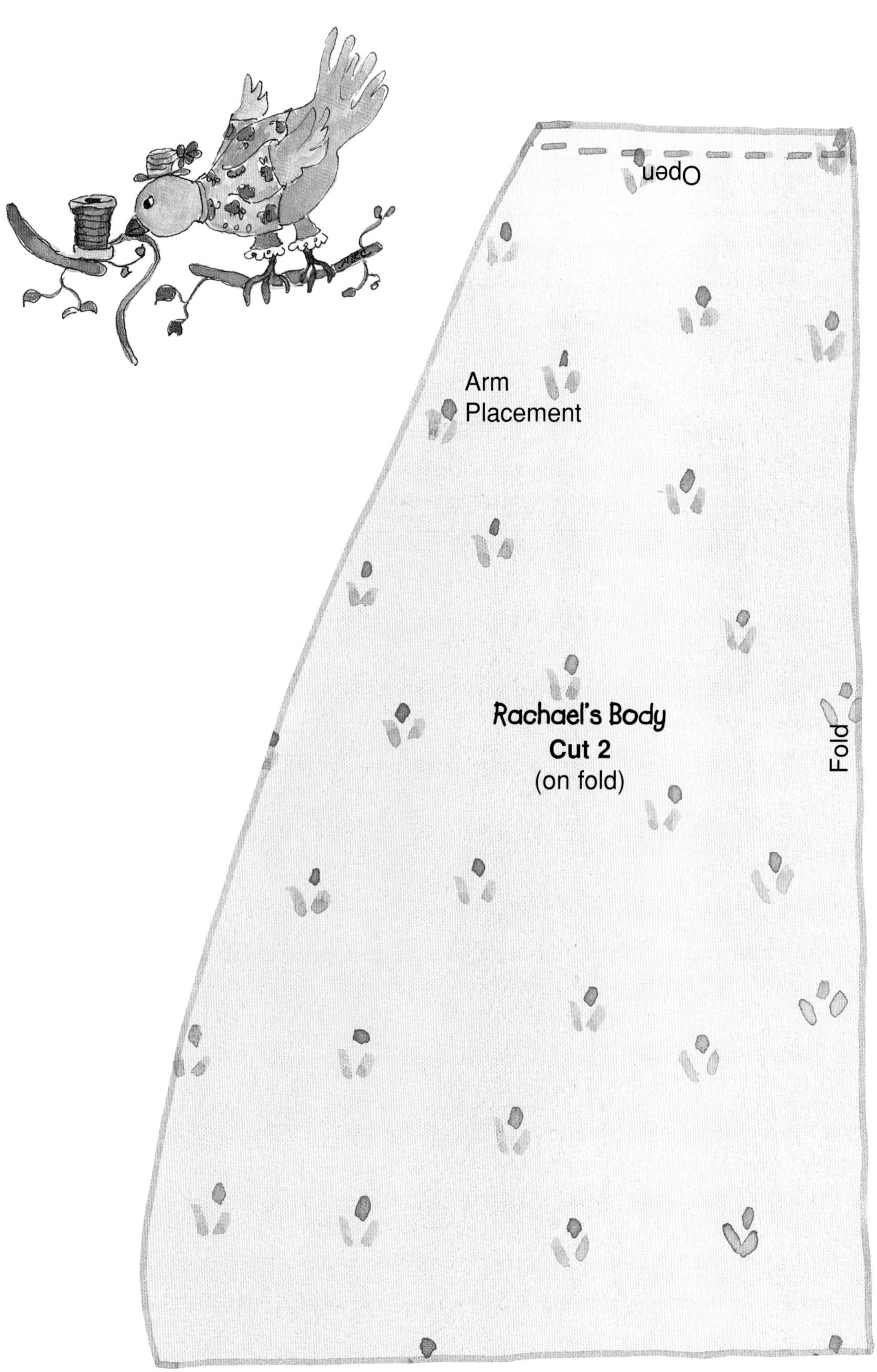
Open
Arm
Placement
Rachael's Body
Cut 2
(on fold)
Fold

Helouise, holding her sewing basket

Helouise, the sewing angel pictured on page 31, is very much like Rachael. Helouise's body is a little bigger and her head has an attitude! Helouise is ready to serve your repair needs by placing a small basket, containing a small sewing kit and scraps of fabric and yarn, in her arms.

Materials

Buttons: medium (2)
Embroidery floss: brown
Eyes: glass or safety, 8 mm, black
Fabrics: felt, muslin, or print, 12" square for wings; felt, synthetic fur, or wool (1/4 yd.) for arms, ears, and head; felt square (scrap) for nose; flannel, printed (1/4 yd.) for body; wool, 6" x 12" for shawl
Lace: 6"-wide
Plastic pellets: (1 cup)
Polyester stuffing: small bag
Ribbon: coordinating color of choice, width of choice (1 yd.)
Sewing kit: small
Straw basket: tiny
Thread: heavy; sewing, coordinating color of choice

Tools

Cardboard
Fabric marker
Measuring tape
Needles: doll, 5" or longer; embroidery; sewing
Pencil
Pins
Scissors: craft; fabric
Sewing machine with thread
Stuffing stick
Tracing paper

All seam allowances are 1/8".

Beginnings

1. Read "Bear Necessities" on pages 8–17 before beginning. Organize all materials and tools needed for this project.

2. Using pencil, tracing paper, cardboard, and craft scissors, make templates of pattern pieces on pages 38–40.

3. Place templates on backs of fabric. Using fabric marker, trace pattern. Using fabric scissors, cut out fabric pieces.

4. Using sewing machine, sew darts in head.

5. Sew head, ear, arm, and wing pieces, with right sides together, leaving open where marked.

6. Sew body pieces, with right sides together, leaving open where marked. Square off bottom corners by folding bottom seam flat and sewing across corners. Check all seams. Turn all sewn pieces right side out.

Note: If using glass eyes, stuff head first. If using safety eyes, insert eyes first and then stuff head.

7. Using stuffing stick, stuff head firmly with polyester stuffing. Stuff arms and wings. Fill bottom of body with plastic pellets, then stuff body firmly to the top with polyester stuffing.

Face

8. Using pins, mark eye placement. Using doll needle, insert eyes onto face with heavy thread.

9. Using pins, attach ears onto head where marked on pattern. See "Ladder Stitch" on page 15. Using embroidery needle, sew ears onto head with heavy thread and Ladder Stitch.

10. Using pencil, trace desired nose pattern from page 14 onto tracing paper, creating template. Using craft scissors, cut out template. Using fabric marker, trace template onto felt. Using fabric scissors, cut out nose piece. Pin felt nose onto face.

11. See "Satin Stitch" on page 15. Using embroidery needle, embroider over felt nose with embroidery floss and Satin Stitch. Embroider mouth.

Arms & Body

12. Using embroidery needle, gather-stitch around opening on body with heavy thread, leaving slightly open to fit base of head. Sew arms closed.

Continued on page 40.

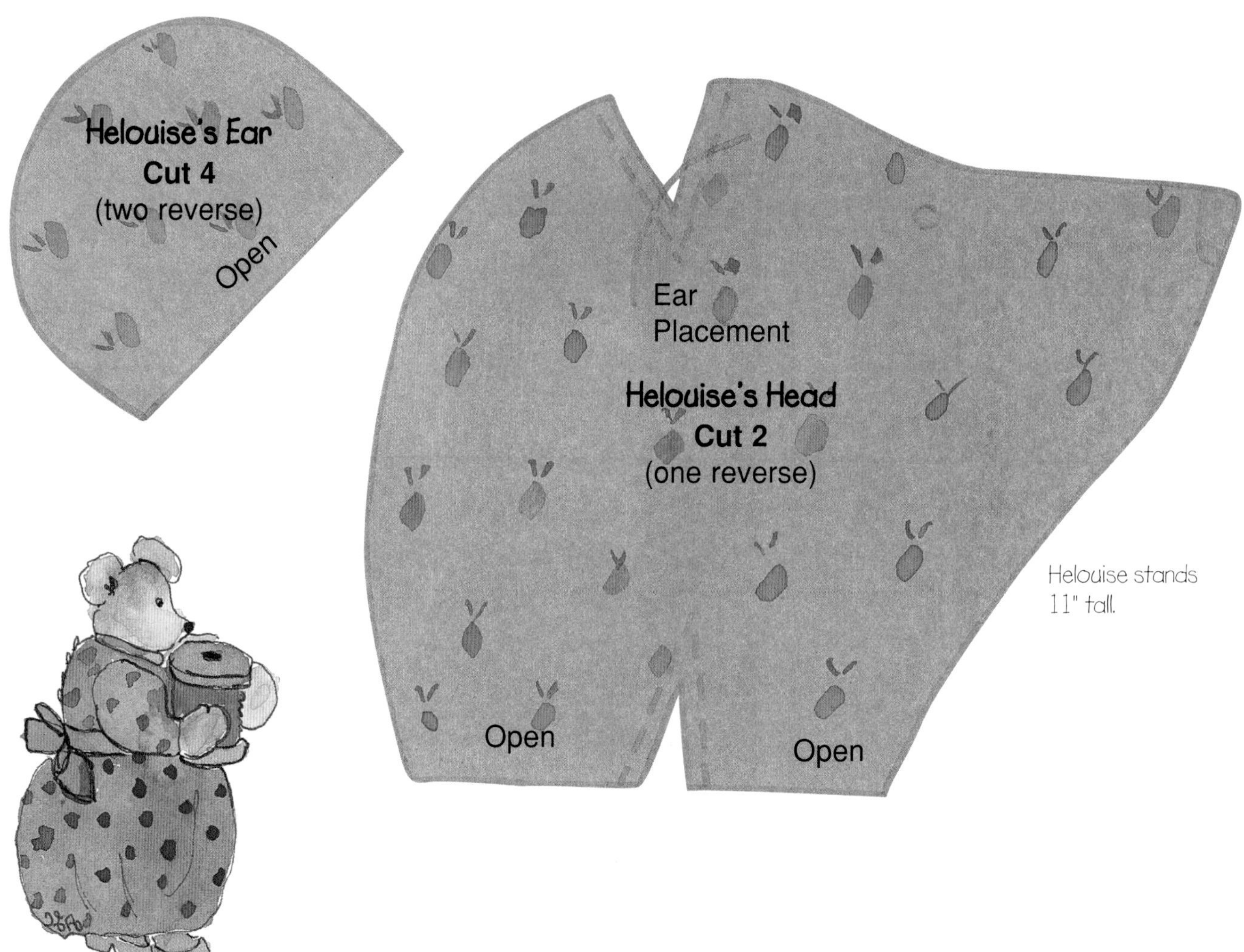

Helouise stands 11" tall.

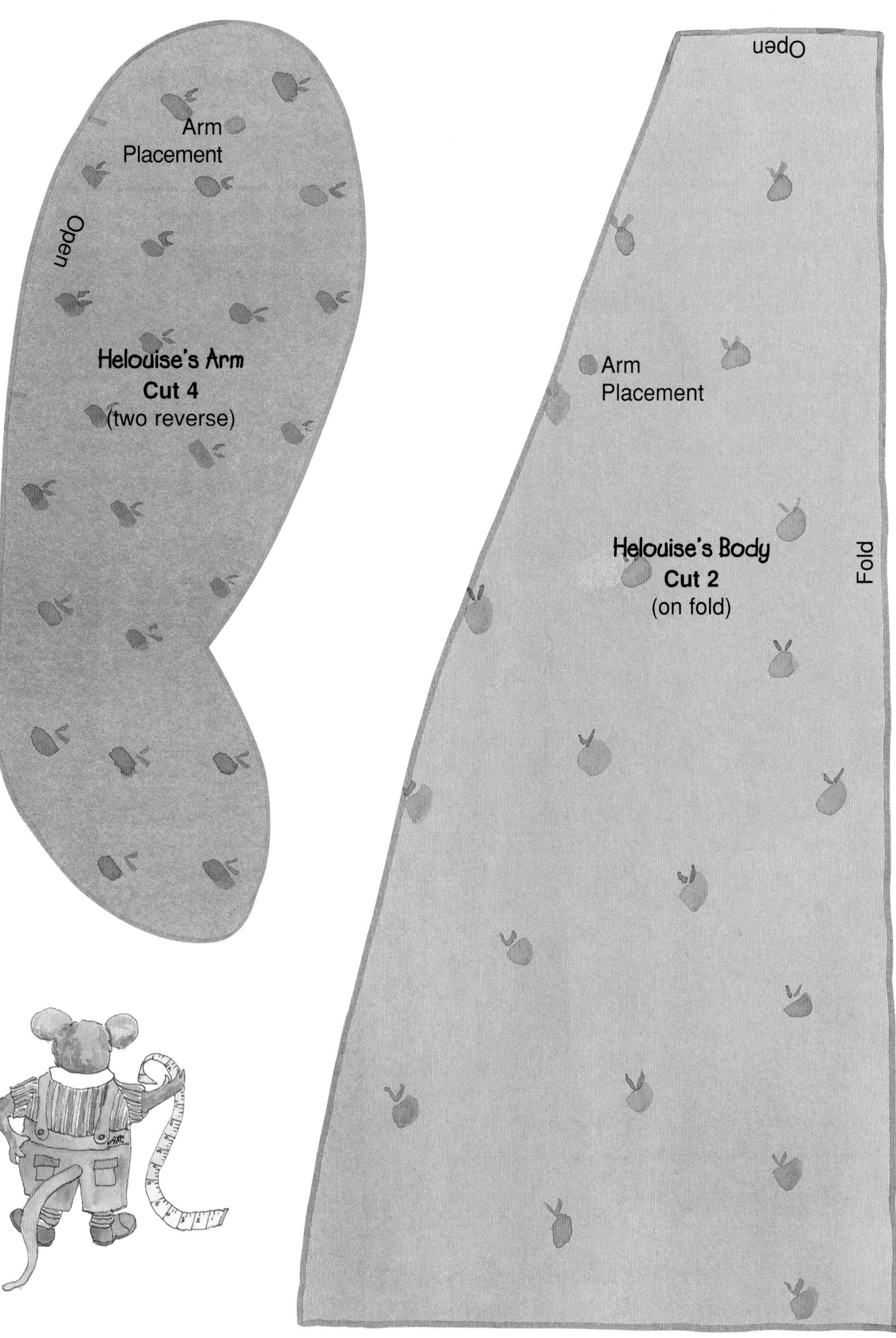
Arm
Placement
Open
Helouise's Arm
Cut 4
(two reverse)
Open
Arm
Placement
Helouise's Body
Cut 2
(on fold)
Fold

Continued from page 38.

13. Using doll needle, sew arms onto body, with heavy thread and buttons.

14. Align center seams of head and body. See "Ladder Stitch" on page 15. Using embroidery needle, sew head onto body with heavy thread and Ladder Stitch. Sew around neck twice for strength.

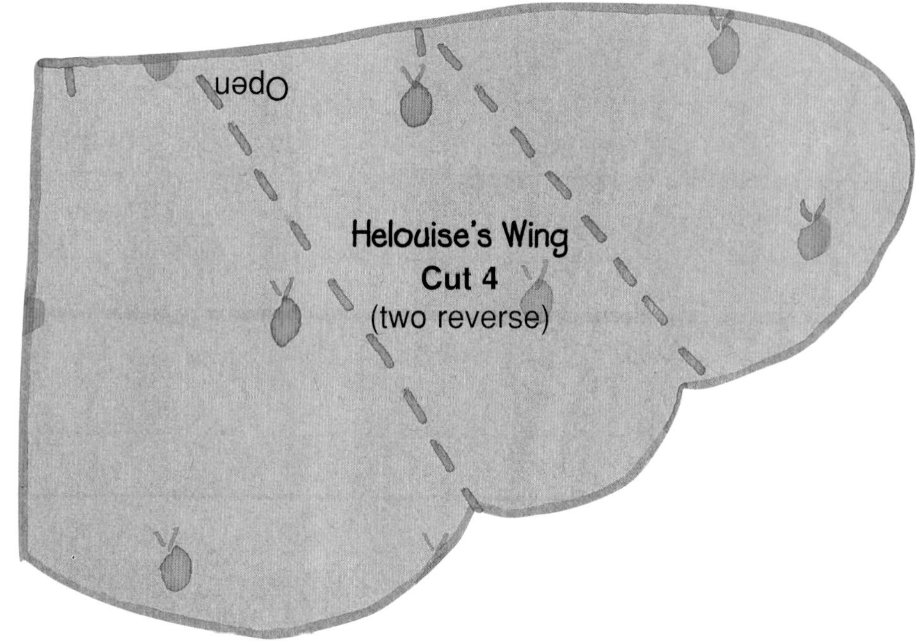

Wings

15. See pattern on right. Dotted lines indicate quilting. Using sewing machine, quilt wings. Sew wings closed.

16. Using embroidery needle, sew wings onto back of bear with embroidery floss.

Apron

17. Place lace scrap around bear's waist. Using sewing needle, tack to secure with sewing thread.

Shawl

18. Wrap wool around shoulders for shawl. Tack to secure with sewing thread.

Finishings

19. Place straw basket in arms. Sew paws to basket. Fill straw basket with small sewing kit, scraps of yarn and fabric, etc.

Helouise before adding clothing

Colette and friend with their pincushions (Instructions for Colette and friend, see page 47.)

Bearheart

I designed "Bearheart" for a friend who was going off to college. She always had her special "blanket or banky" as a small child and still found it very comforting as she grew older. I created a special bear from the blanket so he could travel with her to college. This little bear will always be a special comfort to her. You might want to make this bear for a special friend's birthday, placing a card in his arms.

Materials

Buttons: medium (2)
Embroidery floss: brown
Eyes: glass or safety, 8 mm, black
Fabrics: blanket, felt, or flannel (1/4 yd.) for body; felt square (scrap) for nose; low-loft quilt batting, felt, or synthetic fur (1/4 yd.) for ears and head; print, contrasting color of choice, (scrap) for heart
Polyester stuffing: small bag
Ribbon: coordinating color of choice, 2"-wide
Thread: heavy; sewing, coordinating color of choice

Tools

Cardboard
Fabric marker
Iron
Measuring tape
Needles: doll, 5" or longer; embroidery; sewing
Pencil
Pins
Scissors: craft; fabric
Sewing machine with thread
Stuffing stick
Tracing paper

All seam allowances are 1/8".

Beginnings

1. Read "Bear Necessities" on pages 8–17 before beginning. Organize all materials and tools needed for this project.

2. Using pencil, tracing paper, cardboard, and craft scissors, make templates of pattern pieces on pages 44–46.

3. Place templates on backs of fabric. Using fabric marker, trace pattern. Using fabric scissors, cut out fabric pieces.

4. Using sewing machine, sew head, ear, arm, and heart pieces, with right sides together, leaving open where marked.

5. Sew body pieces, with right sides together, leaving open where marked. Sew around body and legs. Check all seams. Turn all sewn pieces right side out.

Note: If using glass eyes, stuff head first. If using safety eyes, insert eyes first and then stuff head.

6. Using stuffing stick stuff head firmly with polyester stuffing. Stuff arms and heart. Stuff body firmly to top with polyester stuffing.

Face

7. Using pins, mark eye placement. Using doll needle, pull eyes onto face with heavy thread.

8. Using pins, attach ears onto head where marked on pattern. See "Ladder Stitch" on page 15. Using embroidery needle, sew ears onto head with heavy thread and Ladder Stitch.

9. Using pencil, trace desired nose pattern from page 14 onto tracing paper, creating template. Using craft scissors, cut out template. Using fabric marker, trace template onto felt. Using fabric scissors, cut out felt nose. Pin felt nose onto face.

10. See "Satin Stitch" on page 15. Using embroidery needle, embroider over felt nose with embroidery floss and Satin Stitch. Embroider mouth.

Bearheart's Ear
Cut 4
(two reverse)
Open

Bearheart stands 9" tall.

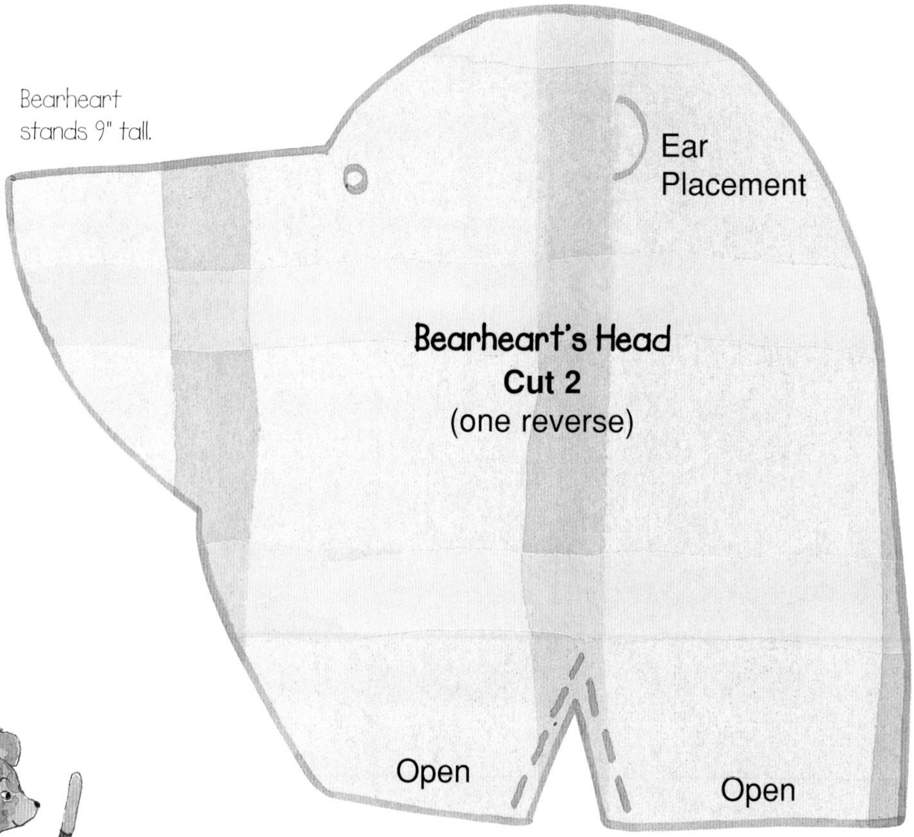

Ear Placement

Bearheart's Head
Cut 2
(one reverse)

Open

Open

Arms & Body

11. Using embroidery needle, gather-stitch around opening on body with heavy thread, leaving slightly open to fit base of head. Sew arms closed.

12. Using doll needle, sew arms onto body 2½" from neck on side seam with heavy thread and buttons.

13. Align center seams of head and body. See "Ladder Stitch" on page 15. Using embroidery needle, sew head onto body with heavy thread and Ladder Stitch. Sew around neck twice for strength.

Bow Tie

14. Using fabric scissors, cut 2" x 4" piece of ribbon for bow tie.

15. Using iron, press ¼" folds on 4" sides of ribbon. Fold ends to center, overlapping ¼". Using sewing needle, sew in place.

16. Using fabric scissors, cut 1½" x 2" piece of scrap fabric for center of bow tie.

17. Using iron, press ¼" folds on 2" sides of cut fabric.

18. Wrap small piece of fabric around center of ribbon. Gather. Using sewing needle, sew in place with sewing thread.

19. Place bow tie on bear's neck. Tack bow to secure with sewing thread.

Heart

20. Using sewing needle, sew heart closed with sewing thread.

Finishings

21. Place heart between paws and sew paws together, securing heart in place.

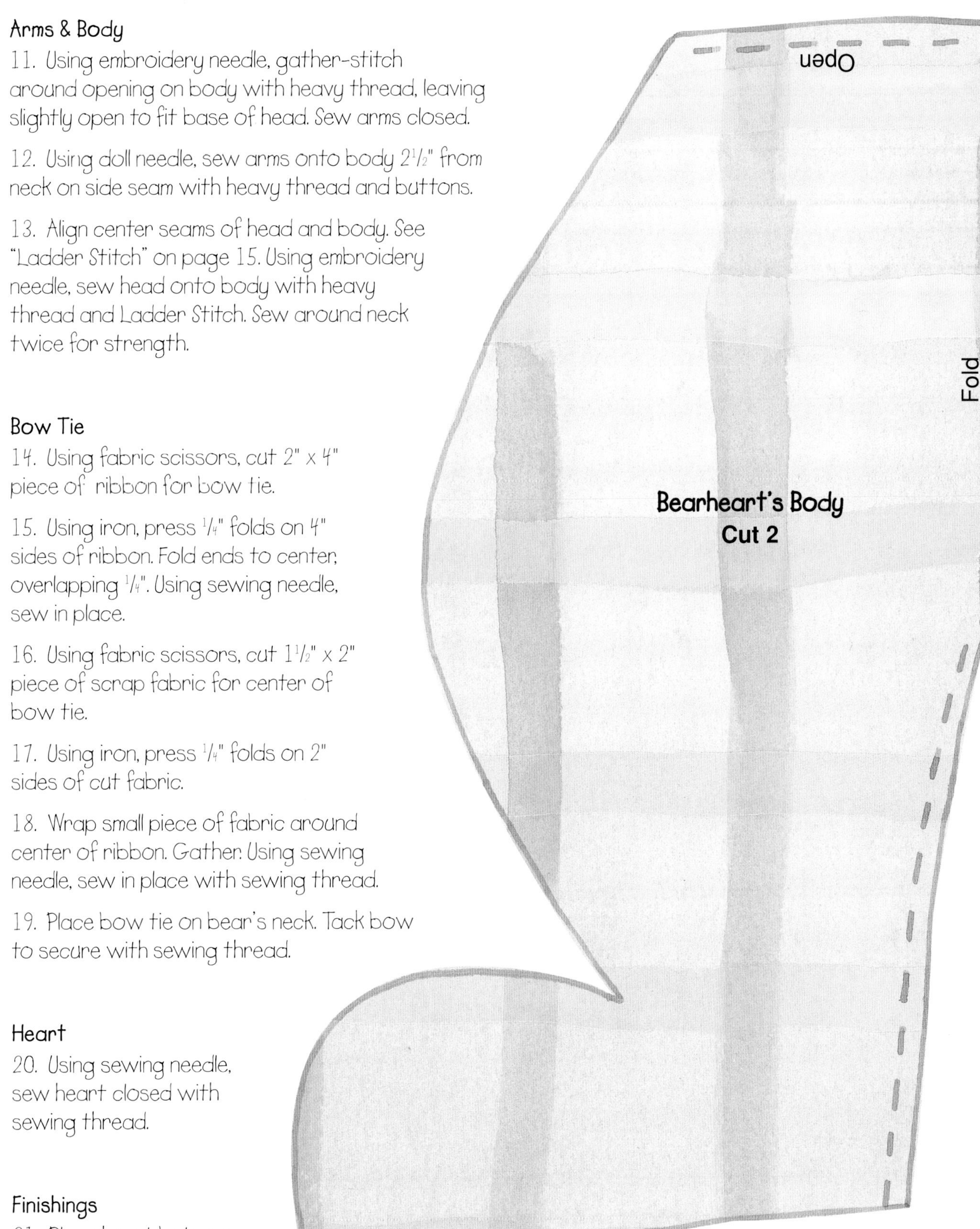

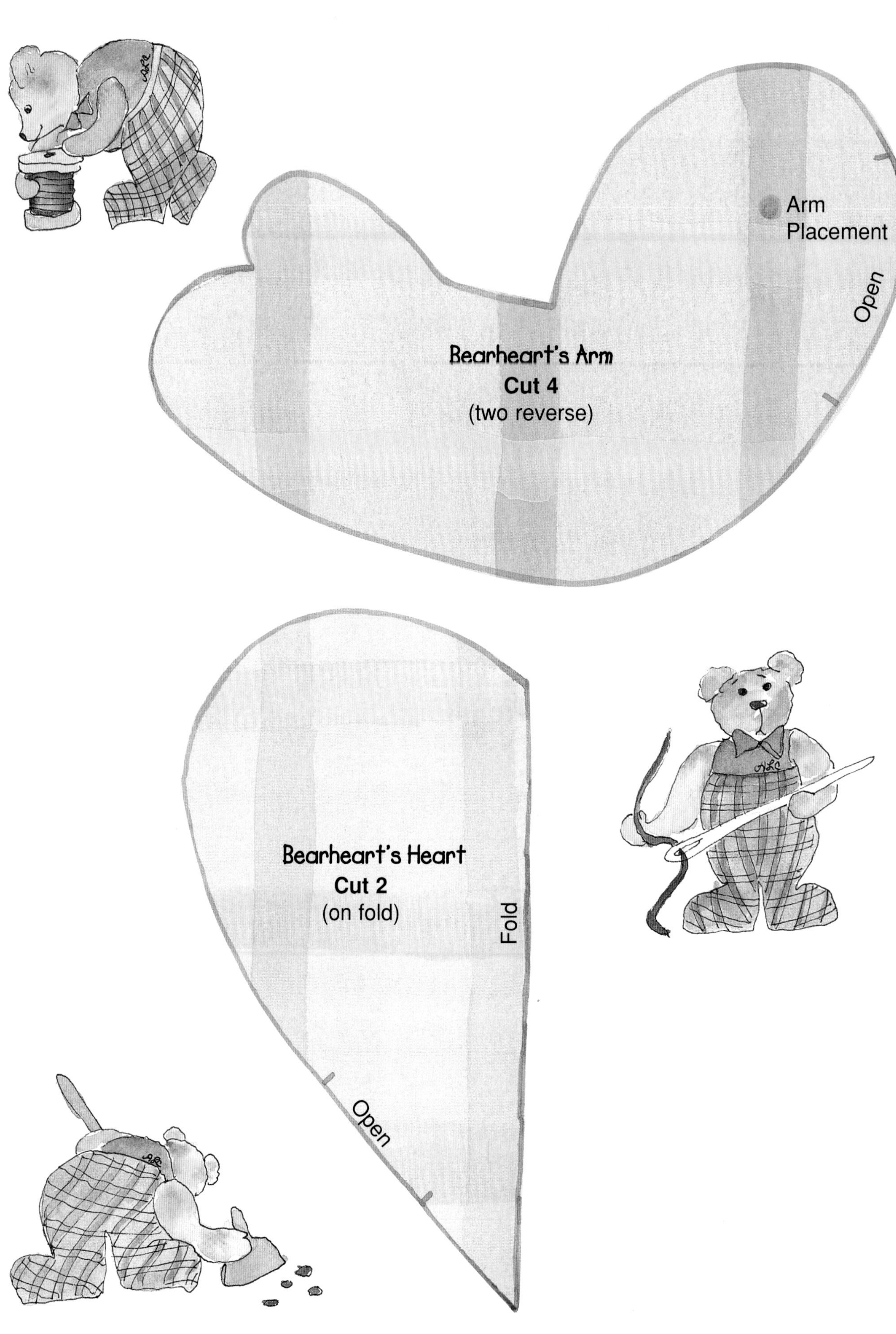
Arm
Placement
Open
Bearheart's Arm
Cut 4
(two reverse)
Bearheart's Heart
Cut 2
(on fold)
Fold
Open

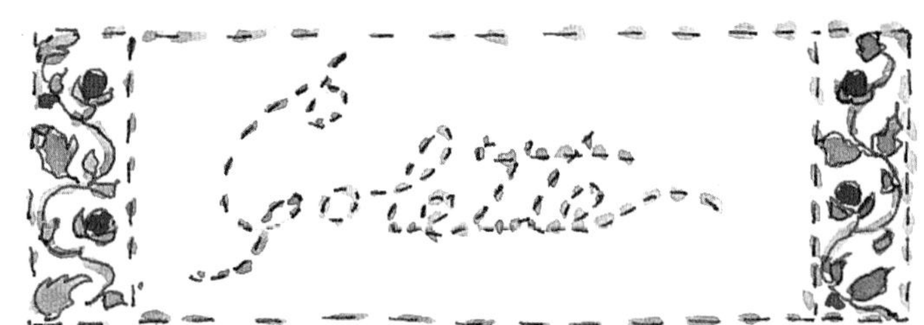

Colette

I designed Colette to hold my pin cushion. She is a wonderful companion next to my sewing machine and welcomes all new bears and animals I create. Colette's head and feet are fur, and her body and arms are cotton fabric. Her skirt is gathered around the waist and is stuffed with batting, to puff it up and fluff around the pin cushion. If you prefer, Colette could sit on the bed without her pin cushion, making her just as charming. Remember to use safety eyes or embroidered eyes if giving this bear to a child.

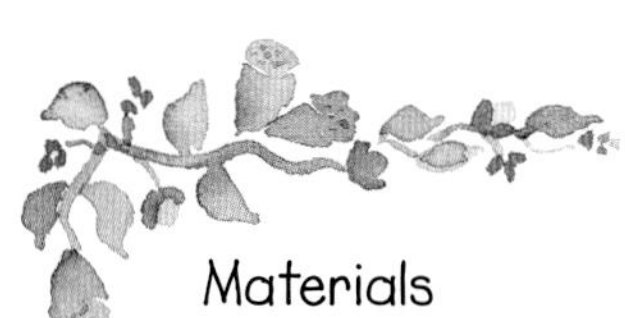

Materials

Buttons: small (2)
Embroidery floss: brown
Eyes: glass or safety, 8 mm, black
Fabrics: felt or synthetic fur (1/4 yd.) for ears and head; felt square (scrap) for nose; lace or loose-weave (scrap) for shawl; print (1/4 yd.) for arms and body, (1/4 yd.) for skirt
Lace: 1/2"-wide (1 yd.)
Pin cushion
Plastic pellets: (1 cup)
Polyester stuffing: small bag
Ribbon: coordinating color of choice; width of choice (1/2 yd.)
Thread: heavy; sewing, coordinating color of choice

Tools

Cardboard
Fabric marker
Needles: doll, 5" or longer; embroidery; sewing
Pencil
Pins
Scissors: craft; fabric
Sewing machine with thread
Stuffing stick
Tracing paper

All seam allowances are 1/8".

Beginnings

1. Read "Bear Necessities" on pages 8–17 before beginning. Organize all materials and tools needed for this project.

2. Using pencil, tracing paper, cardboard, and craft scissors, make templates of pattern pieces on pages 49–50.

3. Place templates on backs of fabric. Using fabric marker, trace pattern. Using fabric scissors, cut out fabric pieces.

4. Using sewing machine, sew darts in head.

5. Sew head, ear, arm, and foot pieces, with right sides together, leaving open where marked.

6. Sew body pieces, with right sides together,

leaving open where marked. Check all seams. Turn all sewn pieces right side out.

Note: If using glass eyes, stuff head first. If using safety eyes, insert eyes first and then stuff head.

7. Using stuffing stick, stuff head firmly with polyester stuffing. Stuff arms and feet. Fill bottom of body with plastic pellets, then stuff body firmly to the top with polyester stuffing.

Face

8. Using pins, mark eye placement. Using doll needle, pull eyes onto face with heavy thread.

9. Using pins, attach ears onto head where marked on pattern. See "Ladder Stitch" on page 15. Using embroidery needle, sew ears onto head with heavy thread and Ladder Stitch.

10. Using pencil, trace desired nose pattern from page 14 onto tracing paper, creating template. Using craft scissors, cut out template. Place template on felt. Using fabric scissors, cut out felt nose. Pin felt nose onto face.

11. See "Satin Stitch" on page 15. Using embroidery needle, embroider over felt nose with embroidery floss and Satin Stitch. Embroider mouth.

Colette stands 13" tall.

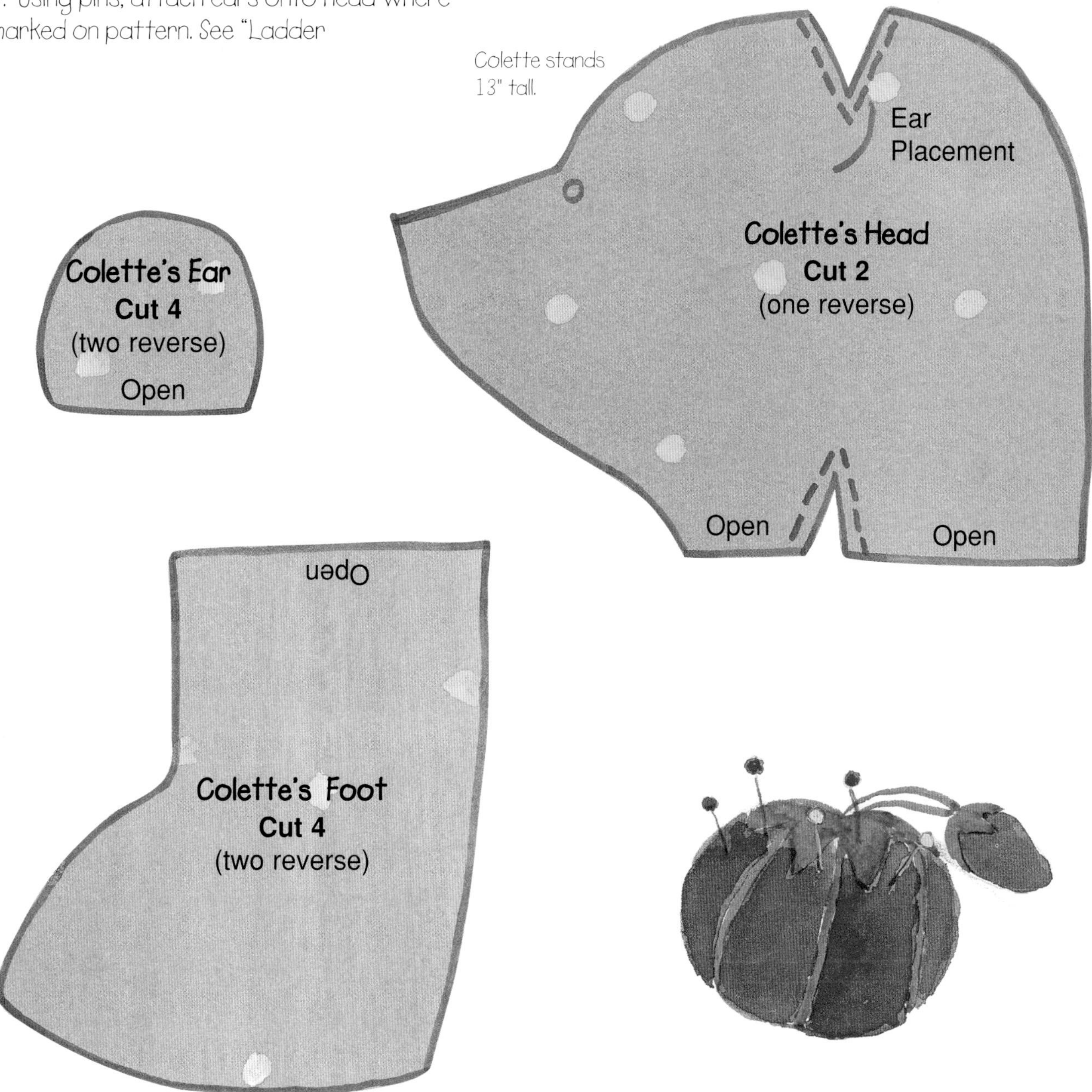

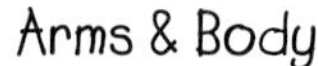

Arms & Body

12. Using embroidery needle, gather-stitch around opening on body with heavy thread, leaving slightly open to fit base of head. Sew arms closed.

13. Using doll needle, sew arms onto body with heavy thread and buttons.

14. Align centers of head and body. See "Ladder Stitch" on page 15. Using embroidery needle, sew head onto body with heavy thread and Ladder Stitch. Sew around neck twice for strength.

Skirt

15. Using sewing machine, gather printed fabric along top long edge to fit around bear's waist. Sew side seam, creating skirt.

16. Slip skirt on bottom of bear. Using embroidery needle, tack onto waist, with raw edges inside skirt, with heavy thread. Pull skirt out. Place a small amount of stuffing inside skirt to fluff.

17. Using pins, attach feet in place at bottom of skirt with toes out or to sides. Using sewing needle, sew feet to skirt with sewing thread.

18. Turn bottom edges of skirt under 1/4". Using sewing machine, sew edges together, from side to side, incorporating feet. Sew lace over stitching.

Shawl

19. Wrap fabric scrap around shoulders for shawl. Using sewing needle, tack to secure with sewing thread. Tack pin cushion in place.

Finishings

20. Tie ribbon around head. Tack in place.

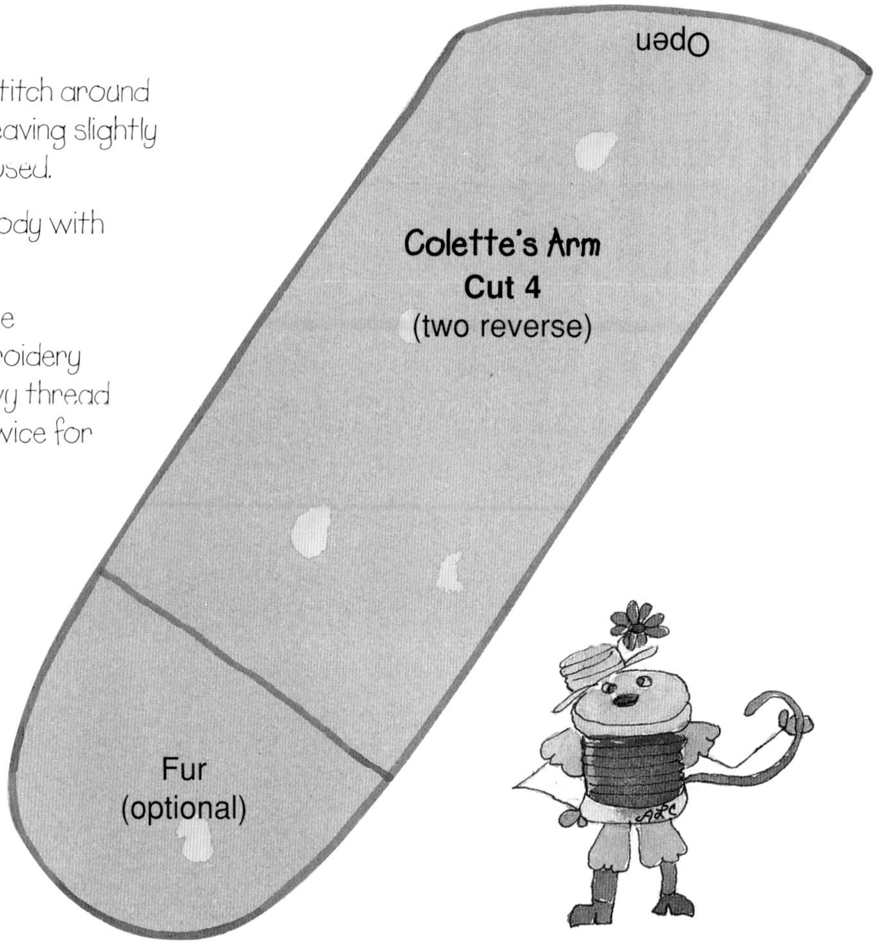

Open

Colette's Arm
Cut 4
(two reverse)

Fur
(optional)

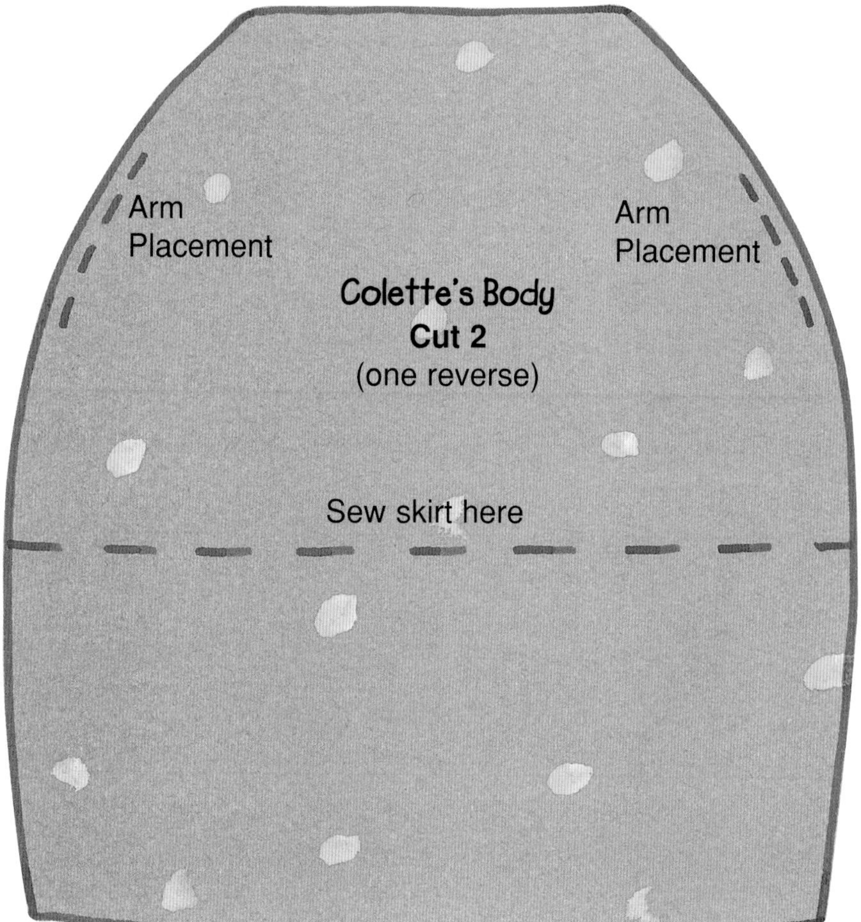

Arm
Placement

Arm
Placement

Colette's Body
Cut 2
(one reverse)

Sew skirt here

Colette and friends in the afternoon sun (Colette's bear friend is made from the same pattern as Colette, just different fur.)

Maggie

Maggie and Mozart are made from the same pattern. They have different ears and a different type of fur. Maggie has a dainty shawl and matching skirt/apron (designed to show her tail). Her eyes are topaz with dark centers. I have fun making these quick and adorable friends.

Materials

Button: small
Embroidery floss: pink
Eyes: glass or safety, 8 mm, topaz with dark center
Fabrics: felt square (scrap) for nose; loose-weave (1/4 yd.) for apron and shawl; low-nap or plush (1/4 yd.); synthetic fur (1/4 yd.) for ears, head, body, and tail
Plastic pellets: (2/3 cup)
Polyester stuffing: small bag
Thread: heavy; sewing, coordinating color of choice

Tools

Cardboard
Fabric marker
Needles: doll, 5" or longer; embroidery; sewing
Pencil
Pins
Scissors: craft; fabric
Sewing machine with thread
Stuffing stick
Tracing paper

All seam allowances are 1/8".

Beginnings

1. Read "Bear Necessities" on pages 8–17 before beginning. Organize all materials and tools needed for this project.

2. Using pencil, tracing paper, cardboard, and craft scissors, make templates of pattern pieces on page 54–55.

3. Place templates on backs of fabric. Using fabric marker, trace patterns. Using fabric scissors, cut out fabric pieces.

4. Using sewing machine, sew head and ear pieces, with right sides together, leaving open where marked.

5. Sew body pieces, with right sides together, leaving open where marked. Check all seams. Turn all sewn pieces right side out.

6. Using embroidery needle, gather-stitch around tail with heavy thread.

Note: If using glass eyes, stuff head first. If using safety eyes, insert eyes first and then stuff head.

7. Using stuffing stick, stuff head firmly with polyester stuffing. Stuff arms and feet, leaving space between each paw and arm and each foot and leg. Stuff tail. Fill bottom of body with plastic pellets, then stuff body lightly to top with polyester stuffing.

Face

8. Using pins, mark eye placement. Using doll needle, pull eyes onto face with heavy thread.

9. Using pins, attach ears onto head where marked on pattern. See "Ladder Stitch" on page 15. Using embroidery needle, sew ears to head with heavy thread and Ladder Stitch.

10. Using pencil, trace desired nose pattern from page 14 onto tracing paper, creating template. Using craft scissors, cut out template. Using fabric marker, trace template onto felt. Using fabric scissors, cut out felt nose. Pin felt nose onto face.

11. See "Satin Stitch" on page 15. Using embroidery needle, embroider over felt nose with embroidery floss and Satin Stitch. Embroider mouth.

Arms, Body, Legs, & Tail

12. Using embroidery needle, gather-stitch around opening on body with heavy thread, leaving slightly open to fit base of head.

13. Sew across where arms and legs meet body.

14. Align center seams of head and body. See "Ladder Stitch" on page 15. Using embroidery needle, sew head onto body with heavy thread and Ladder Stitch. Sew around neck twice for strength.

15. Pull gathering threads on tail to close. See "Ladder Stitch" on page 15. Sew tail onto back of bunny with embroidery floss and Ladder Stitch.

16. Fold arms and legs to front of body. Using sewing needle, tack to secure with sewing thread.

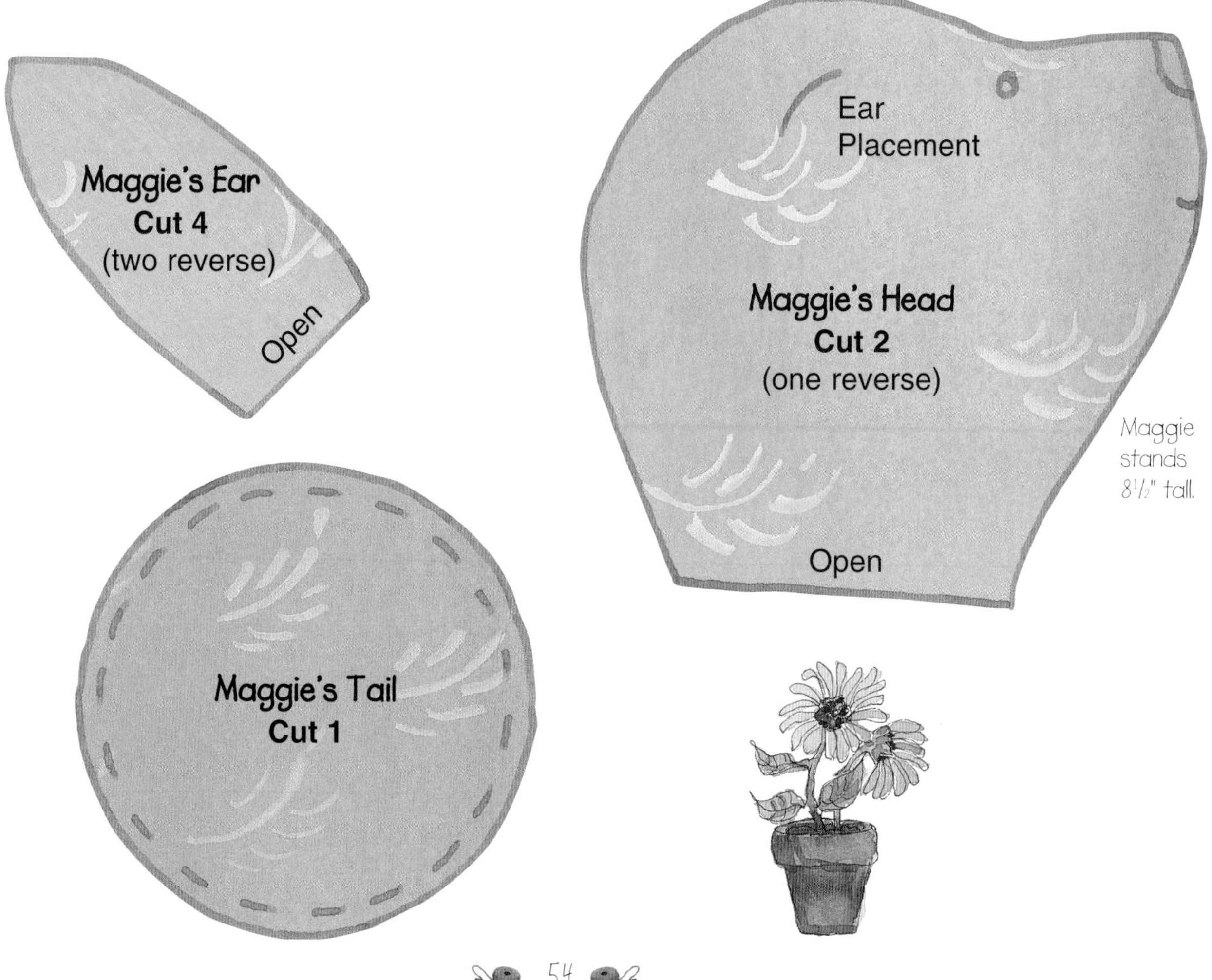

Maggie stands 8½" tall.

♥ See completed bear on page 56 before adding clothing.

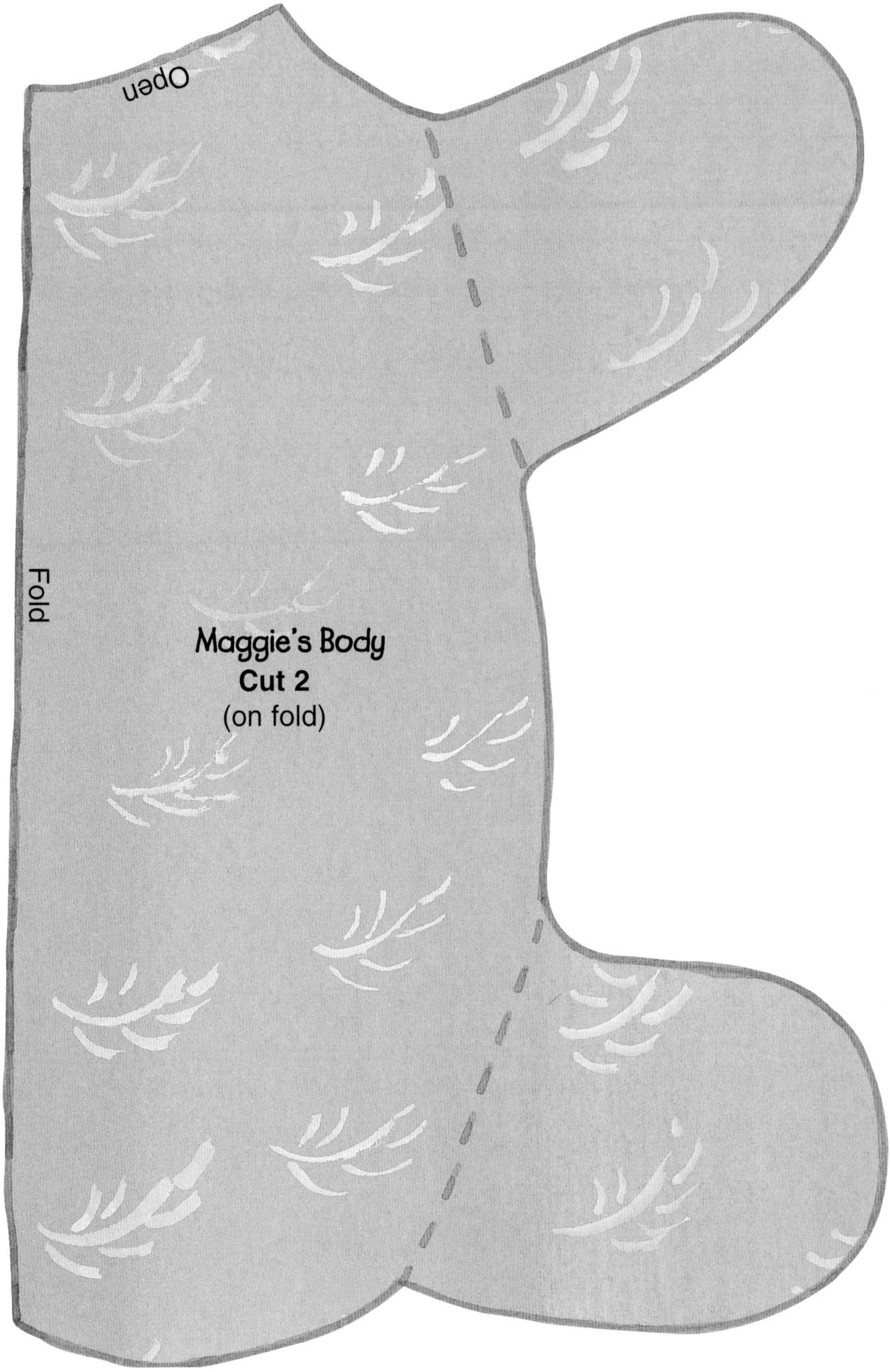

Apron

17. Using fabric scissors, cut 5" x 14" piece of loose-weave fabric.

18. Using sewing needle, pull threads out along all edges to create fringe.

19. Using sewing machine, gather-stitch top long edge.

20. Using fabric scissors, cut 2" x 22" piece of loose-weave fabric for sash. Center sash on top of gather and sew, leaving ends free on sides for apron ties. Tie apron around bunny's waist.

Shawl

21. Using fabric scissors, cut 5" x 14" piece of loose-weave fabric.

22. Using sewing needle, pull threads out along all edges to create fringe.

23. Wrap shawl around shoulders. Tack to secure with sewing thread

Finishings

24. See portrait on page 53 for button placement. Sew small button on shawl.

Open

Fold

Maggie's Body
Cut 2
(on fold)

Maggie before adding clothing

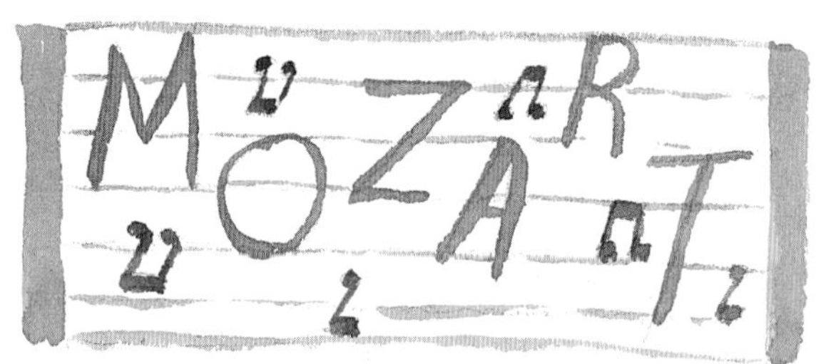

Mozart

Mozart and Maggie are made from the same pattern. They have different ears and a different type of fur. Mozart looks spiffy in his cute vest and jacket. His eyes are black and I added a tail to make him just as cute from the back. Have fun making these quick and adorable characters.

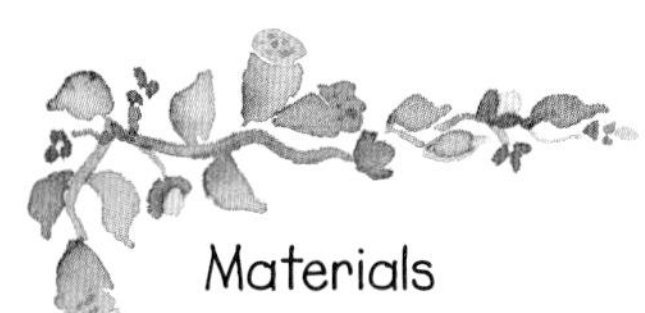

Materials

Buttons: medium (2); small (3)
Embroidery floss: brown
Eyes: glass or safety, 7 mm, black
Fabrics: felt (1/8 yd.) for vest; felt or wool (1/8 yd.) for coat; felt square (scrap) for nose; synthetic fur, low-nap or plush fur (1/4 yd.) for ears, body, head, and tail; (scrap) for bow tie
Plastic pellets: (2/3 cup)
Polyester stuffing: small bag
Thread: heavy; sewing, coordinating color of choice

Tools

Cardboard
Fabric marker
Iron
Needles: doll, 5" or longer; embroidery; sewing
Pencil
Pins
Scissors: craft; fabric
Sewing machine with thread
Stuffing stick
Tracing paper

All seam allowances are 1/8".

Beginnings

1. Read "Bear Necessities" on pages 8–17 before beginning. Organize all materials and tools needed for this project.

2. Using pencil, tracing paper, cardboard, and craft scissors, make templates of pattern pieces on pages 54–55 (do not trace ear) and 59–61.

3. Place templates on backs of fabric. Using fabric marker, trace pattern. Using fabric scissors, cut out fabric pieces.

4. Using sewing machine, sew head and ear pieces, with right sides together, leaving open where marked.

5. Sew body pieces, with right sides together, leaving open where marked. Check all seams. Turn all sewn pieces right side out.

6. Using embroidery needle, gather-stitch around tail with heavy thread.

Note: If using glass eyes, stuff head first. If using safety eyes, insert eyes first and then stuff head.

7. Using stuffing stick, stuff head firmly with polyester stuffing. Stuff arms and feet, leaving space between each paw and arm and each foot and leg. Stuff tail. Fill bottom of body with plastic pellets, then stuff body lightly to top with polyester stuffing.

Mozart stands 8½" high.

Face

8. Using pins, mark eye placement. Using doll needle, pull eyes onto face with heavy thread.

9. Using pins, attach ears onto head where marked on pattern. See "Ladder Stitch" on page 15. Using embroidery needle, sew ears onto head with heavy thread and Ladder Stitch.

10. Using pencil, trace desired nose pattern from page 14 onto tracing paper, creating template. Using craft scissors, cut out template. Using fabric marker, trace template onto felt. Using fabric scissors, cut out felt nose. Pin felt nose onto face.

11. See "Satin Stitch" on page 15. Using embroidery needle, embroider over felt nose with embroidery floss and Satin Stitch. Embroider mouth.

Arms, Body, Legs, & Tail

12. Using embroidery needle, gather-stitch around opening on body with heavy thread, leaving slightly open to fit base of head.

13. Sew across where arms and legs meet body.

14. Align center seams of head and body. See "Ladder Stitch" on page 15. Using embroidery needle, sew head onto body with heavy thread and Ladder Stitch. Sew around neck twice for strength.

15. Pull gathering threads on tail to close. See "Ladder Stitch" on page 15. Sew tail onto back of bear with embroidery floss and Ladder Stitch.

Does your thread match?

16. Fold arms and legs to front of body. Using sewing needle, tack to secure with sewing thread.

Coat & Vest

17. Using sewing machine, sew shoulder seams, with right sides together, on coat. Ease sleeves into sleeve openings, pin, and sew.

18. Sew coat closed from wrist on sleeve to bottom of coat on each side.

19. Sew vest shoulder seams, with right sides together, on vest.

20. Sew vest closed from bottom to top on each side.

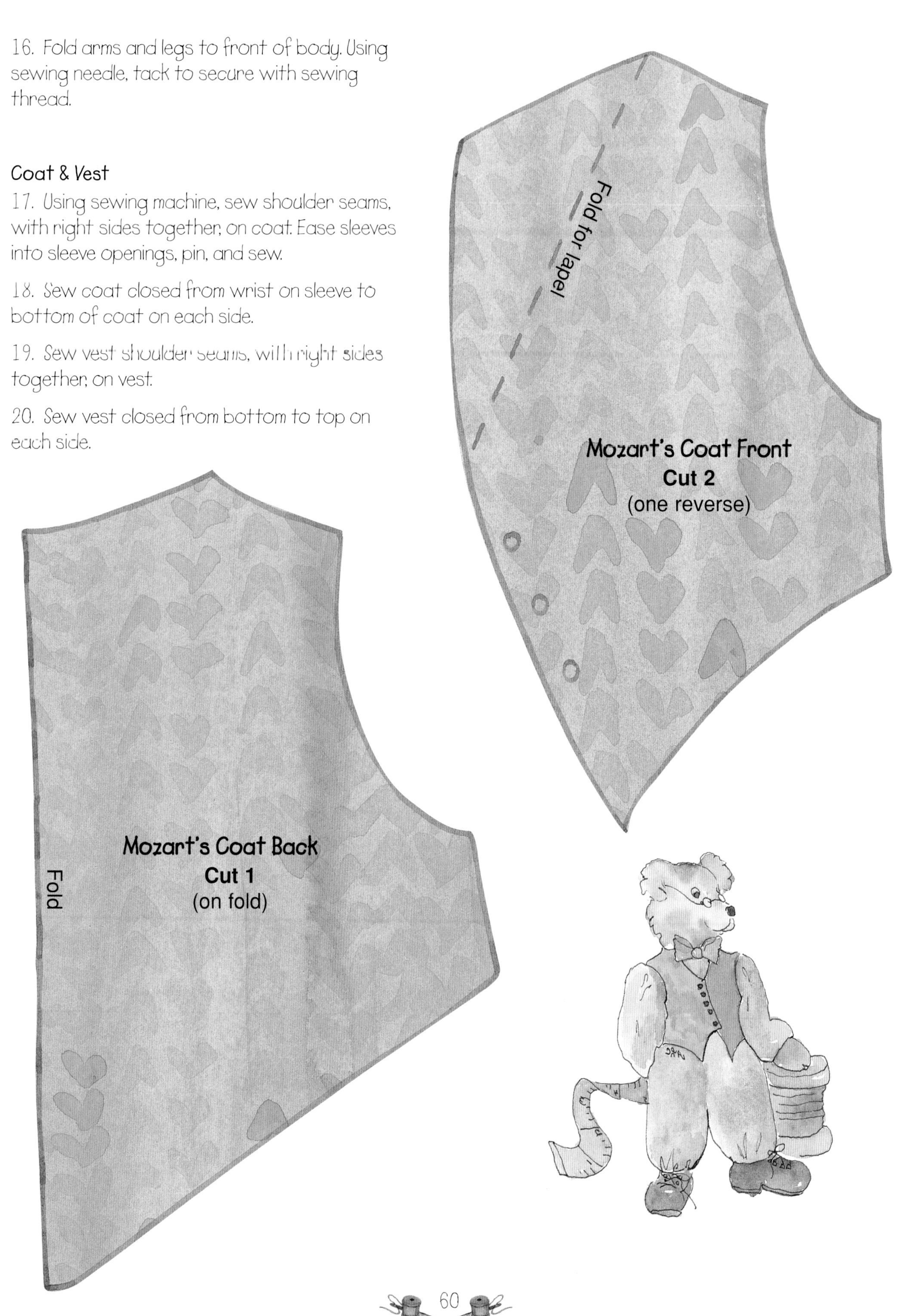

21. See photo on page 57 for button placement. Using sewing needle, sew buttons onto front of coat and vest with sewing thread.

22. Place coat and vest on bear.

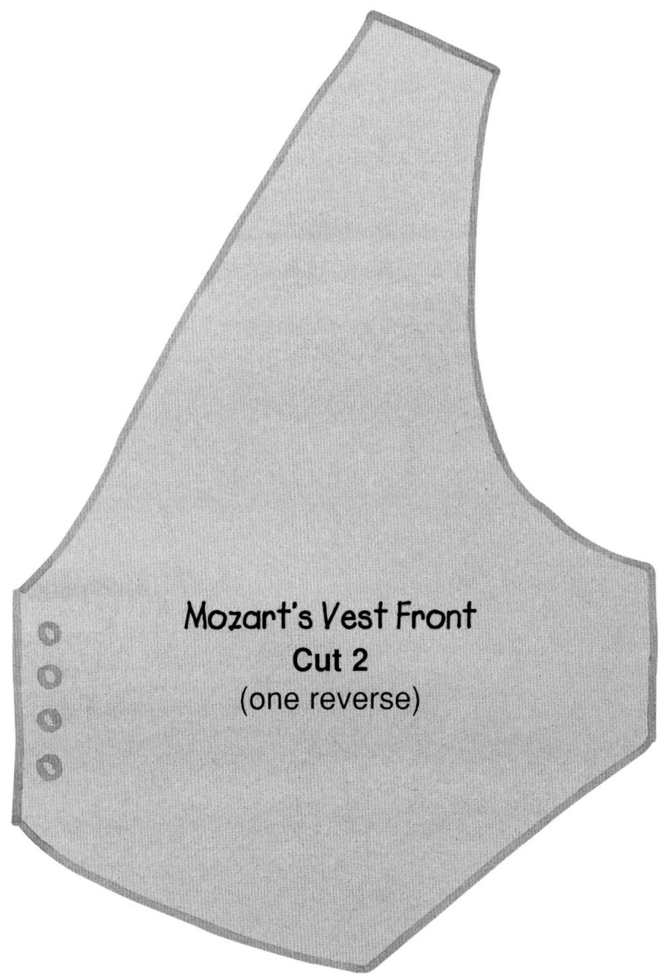

Bow Tie

23. Using fabric scissors, cut 2" x 4" piece of scrap fabric.

24. Using iron, press 1/4" folds on 4" sides of cut fabric.

25. Fold ends to center, overlapping 1/4". Using sewing needle, sew in place.

26. Using fabric scissors, cut 1½" x 2" piece of scrap fabric.

27. Using iron, press 1/4" folds on 2" sides of cut fabric.

28. Wrap small piece of fabric around center of larger piece of fabric. Gather. Using sewing needle, sew in place with sewing thread.

29. Place bow tie on bear's neck. Tack bow to secure with sewing thread.

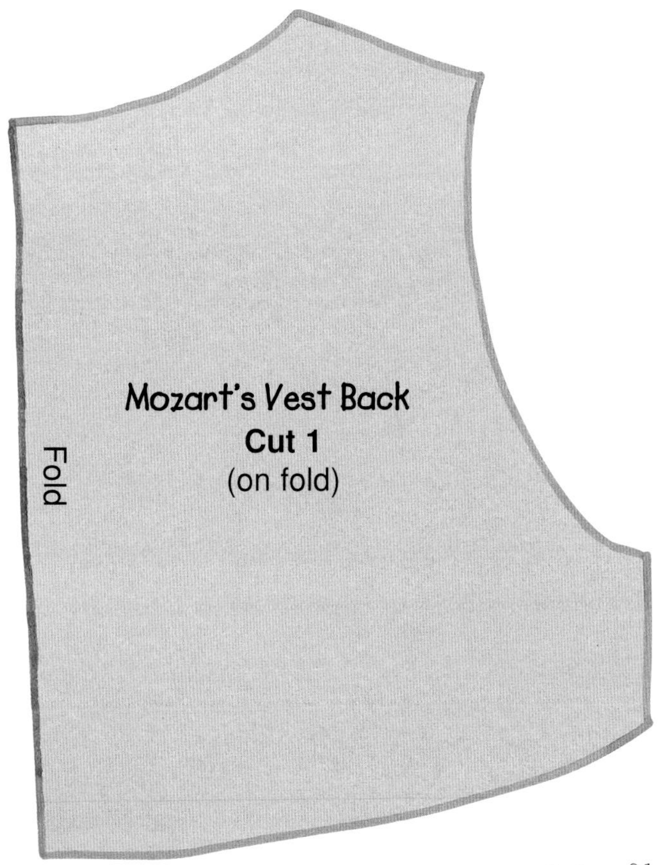

Rose, having tea

I designed Rose in honor of my mother, Rose. She lived at the edge of a winding river in a little cottage for many years. All she had for heat was an antique wood stove that she kept fired up most of the time. She always had fresh baked apple turnovers or pound cake made with large goose eggs baking in the oven. She was the dearest, sweetest old lady in town. Guests never left her house empty handed. She is missed dearly by many and she made our lives full of love and joy. Whenever she went out, she always wore her finest dress, hat, and always her stockings.

Materials

Buttons: medium (4)
Embroidery floss: brown
Eyes: glass or safety, 8 mm, black
Fabrics: felt square (scrap) for nose; mohair or synthetic fur (1/4 yd.) for arms, ears, head/body, and legs; print (1/4 yd.) for dress; wool (1/4 yd.) for coat and hat
Lace: (scrap)
Polyester stuffing: small bag
Ribbon: coordinating color of choice, width of choice (1 yd.)
Snaps: small (2)
Thread: heavy; sewing, coordinating color of choice

Tools

Cardboard
Fabric marker
Needles: doll, 5" or longer; embroidery; sewing
Pencil
Pins
Scissors: craft; fabric
Sewing machine with thread
Stuffing stick
Tracing paper

All seam allowances are 1/8".

Beginnings

1. Read "Bear Necessities" on pages 8–17 before beginning. Organize all materials and tools needed for this project.

2. Using pencil, tracing paper, cardboard, and craft scissors, make templates of pattern pieces on pages 65–70.

3. Place templates on backs of fabric. Using fabric marker, trace pattern. Using fabric scissors, cut out fabric pieces.

4. Using sewing machine, sew darts in head/body.

5. Sew head/body and ear pieces, with right sides together, leaving open where marked.

6. Fold arm and leg pieces over, with right sides together. Sew around pieces, leaving open where marked. Check seams. Turn all sewn pieces right side out.

Note: If using glass eyes, stuff head first. If using safety eyes, insert eyes first and then stuff head.

7. Using stuffing stick, stuff head/body firmly with polyester stuffing. Stuff arms and legs.

8. See "Ladder Stitch" on page 15. Using embroidery needle, sew head/body closed with embroidery floss and Ladder Stitch.

Face

9. Using pins, mark eye placement. Using doll needle, pull eyes onto face with heavy thread.

10. Using pins, attach ears onto head where marked on pattern. See "Ladder Stitch" on page 15. Using embroidery needle, sew ears onto head with heavy thread and Ladder Stitch.

Continued on page 67.

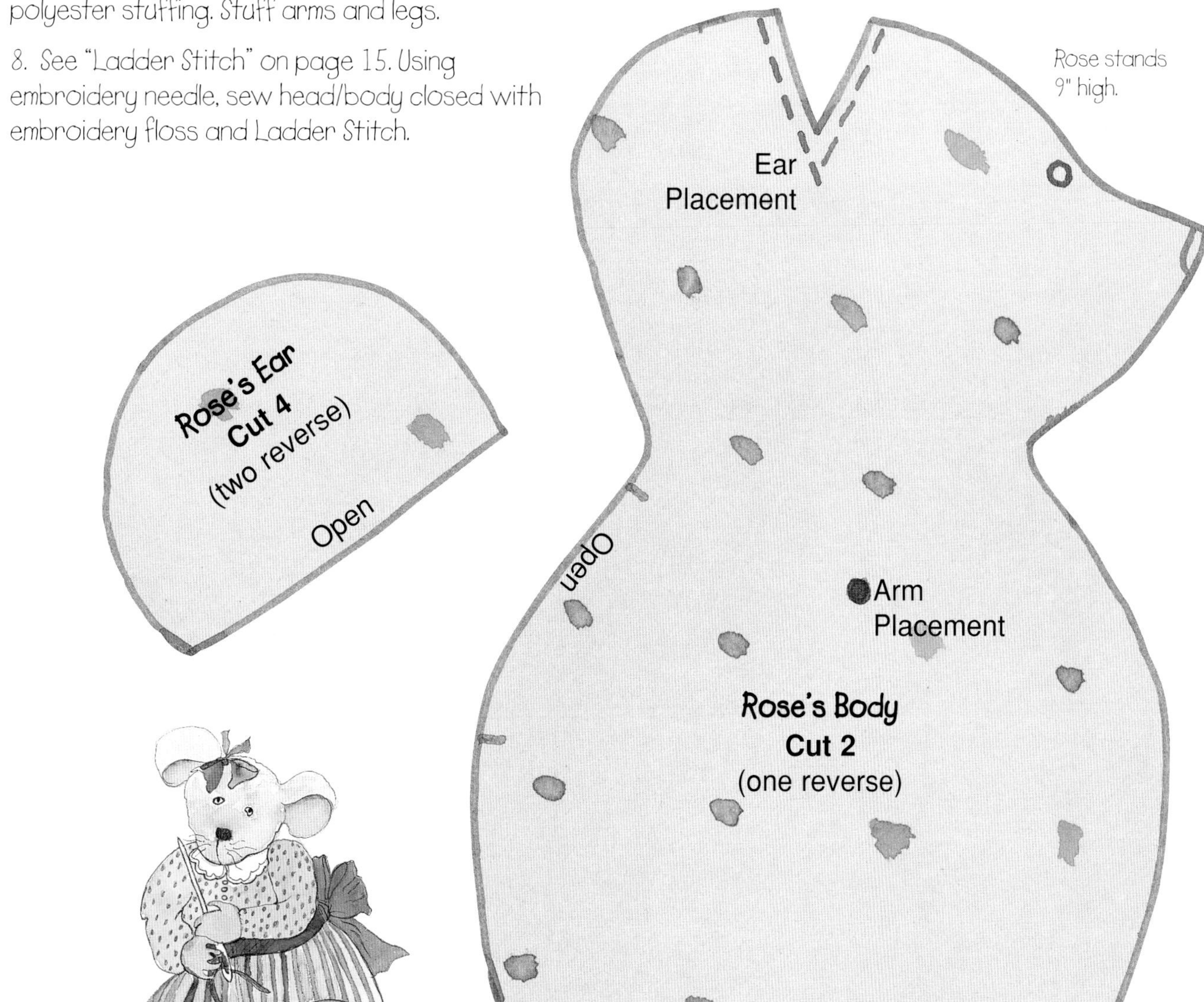

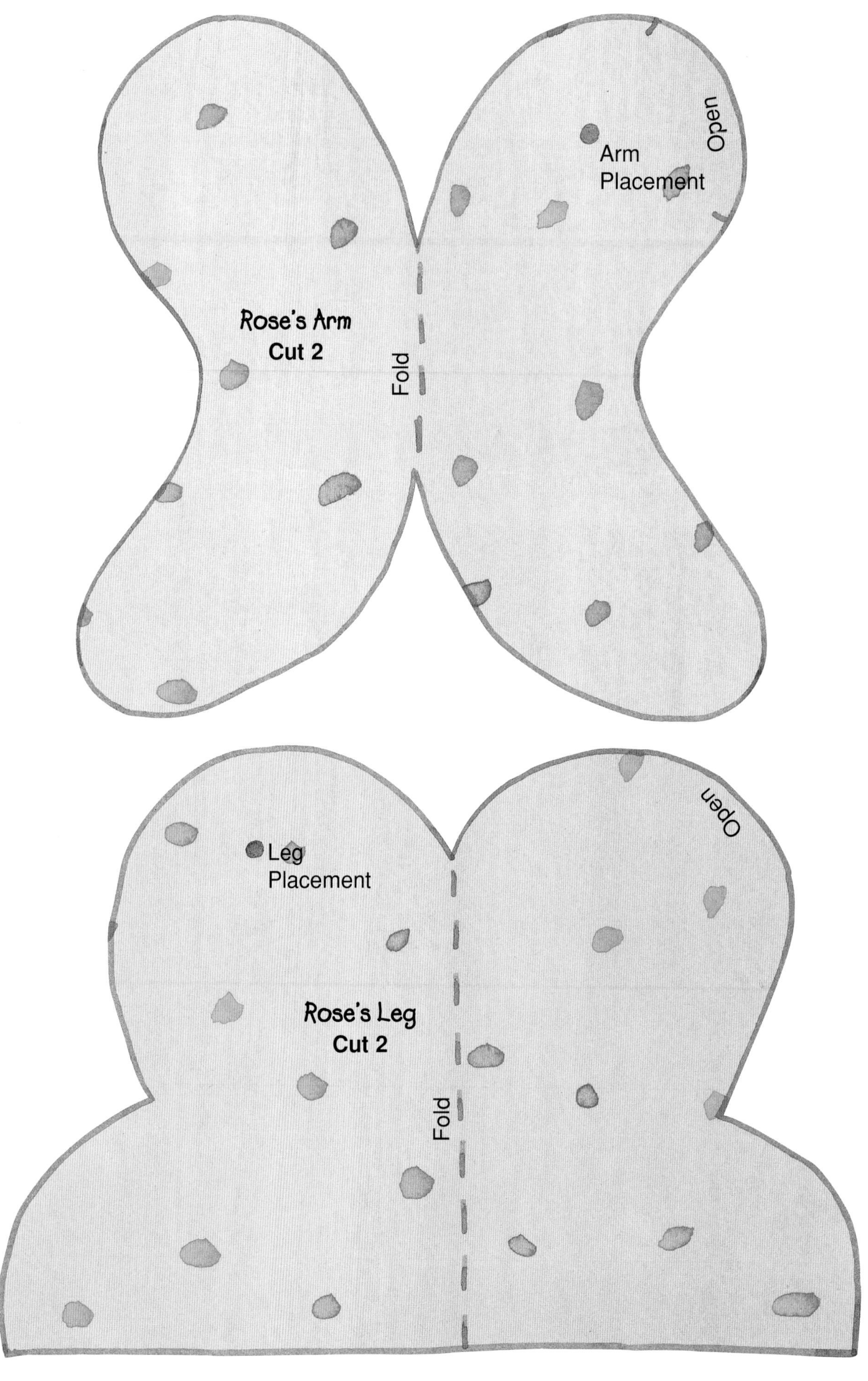
Open
Arm
Placement
Rose's Arm
Cut 2
Fold
Open
Leg
Placement
Rose's Leg
Cut 2
Fold

Continued from page 65.

11. Using pencil, trace desired nose pattern from page 14 onto tracing paper, creating template. Using craft scissors, cut out template. Using fabric marker, trace template onto felt. Using fabric scissors, cut out felt nose. Pin felt nose onto face.

12. See "Satin Stitch" on page 15. Using embroidery needle, embroider over felt nose with embroidery floss and Satin Stitch. Embroider mouth.

Arms, Head/Body, & Legs

13. Using embroidery needle, sew head and body closed with heavy thread. Sew arms and legs closed.

14. Using doll needle, sew arms and legs onto body with heavy thread and buttons.

Dress

15. Using fabric scissors, cut 8" x 19" piece of print fabric for skirt.

16. Using sewing machine, gather-stitch top long edge of skirt.

17. Sew shoulder seams, with right sides together, on dress. Turn down neck edge 1/8" and hem.

18. Turn up sleeve cuff and hem. Ease sleeves in sleeve openings. Sew under arms and side seams, creating bodice.

19. Sew gathered skirt to bodice.

20. Hem 2½" on skirt bottom.

21. Sew up back seam to 1" from waist. Fold edge of opening in and sew ¼".

22. Using sewing needle, sew snaps along edge with sewing thread.

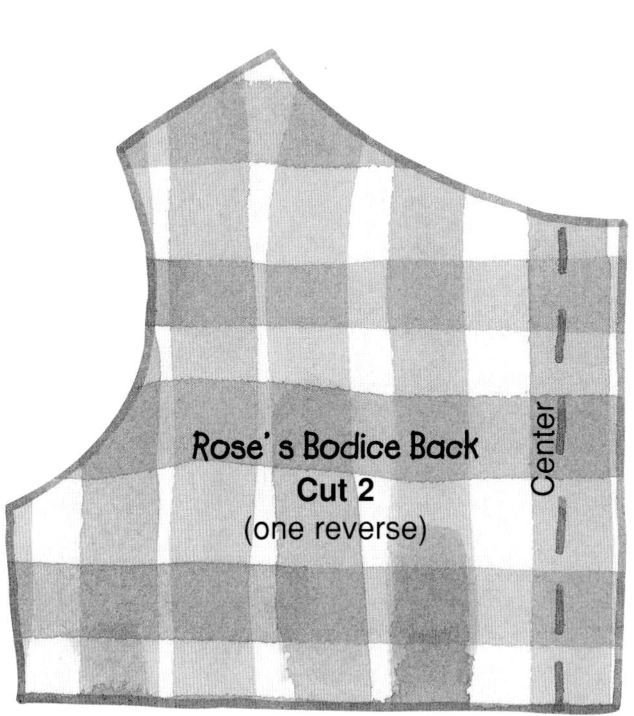

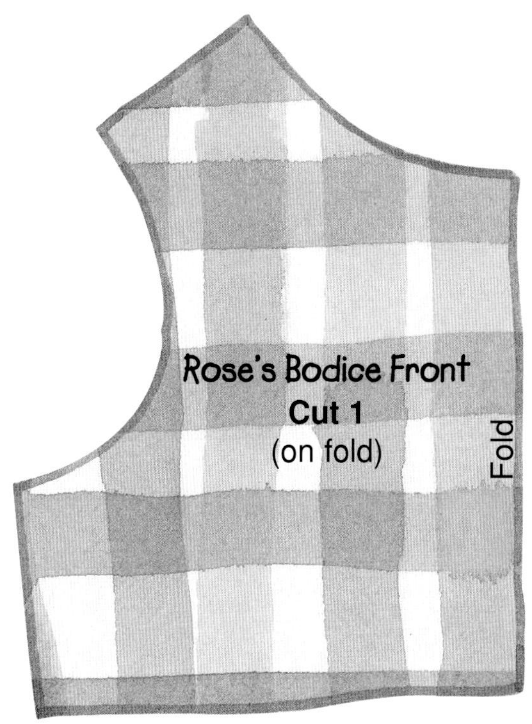

Coat

Lining jacket is optional. See coat on page 70, which is not lined. If you wish to line coat, using contrasting fabric, trace and cut four fronts and two backs. Do not line sleeves. Side seams can be finished, using sewing machine with zig-zag stitch.

23. Using sewing machine, sew shoulder seams, with right sides together, on coat. Ease sleeves into sleeve openings, pin, and sew.

24. Sew coat closed from wrist on sleeve to bottom of coat on each side.

25. Place coat on bear. Fold lapel back.

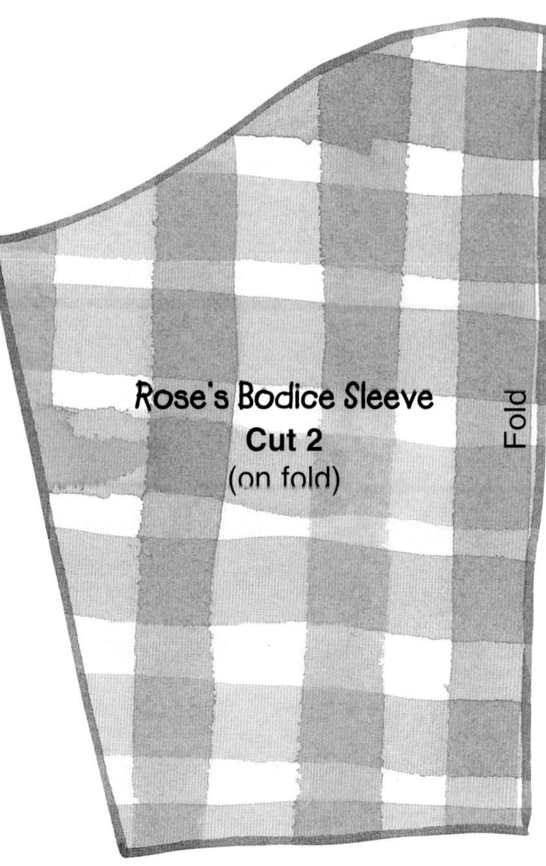

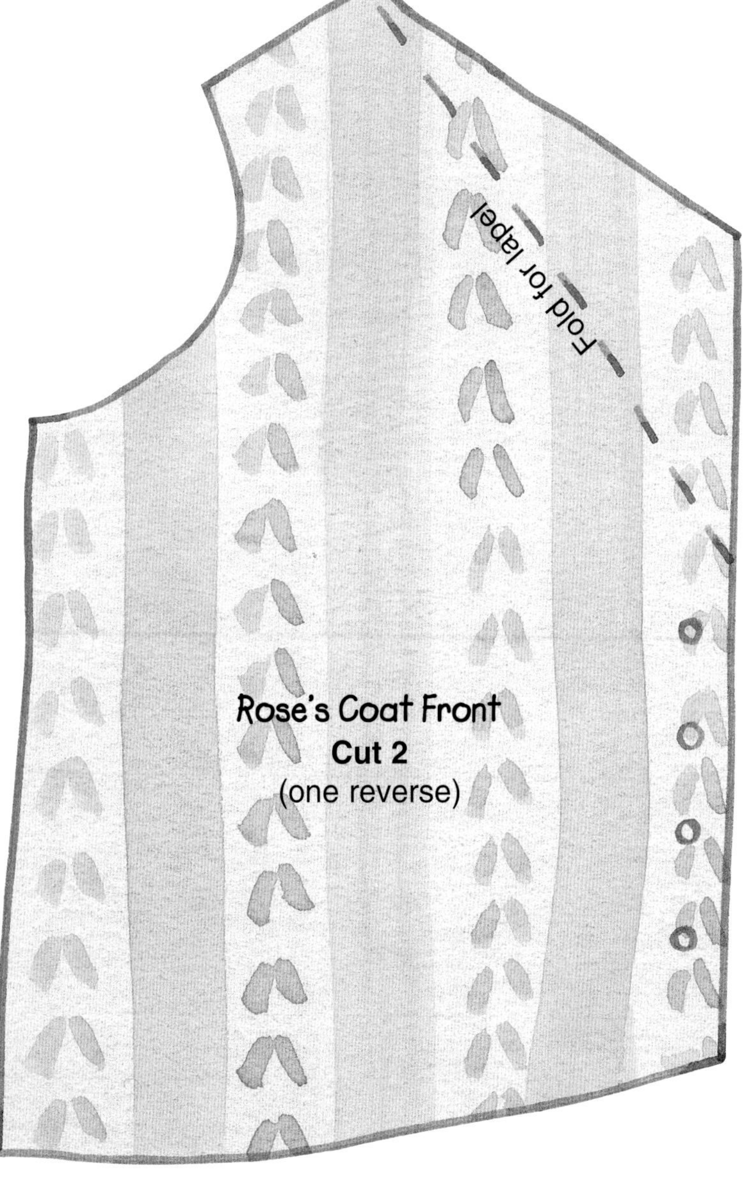

Buttons can be added to finished coat as pattern shows, if desired.

Hat

26. Fold hat band in half, with right sides together. Using sewing machine, sew short ends of hat band together, creating a tube-shape.

27. Place hat top, with wrong side up, on top edge of hat band. Using pins, pin in place. Using sewing needle, sew all the way around with sewing thread. Turn right side out.

28. Sew hat brim onto bottom edge of hat band, with right sides together. Sew brim opening closed.

29. Make bow out of ribbon. Using sewing needle, tack ribbon bow onto front of hat with sewing thread to secure.

30. Tack hat onto bear's head with sewing thread to secure.

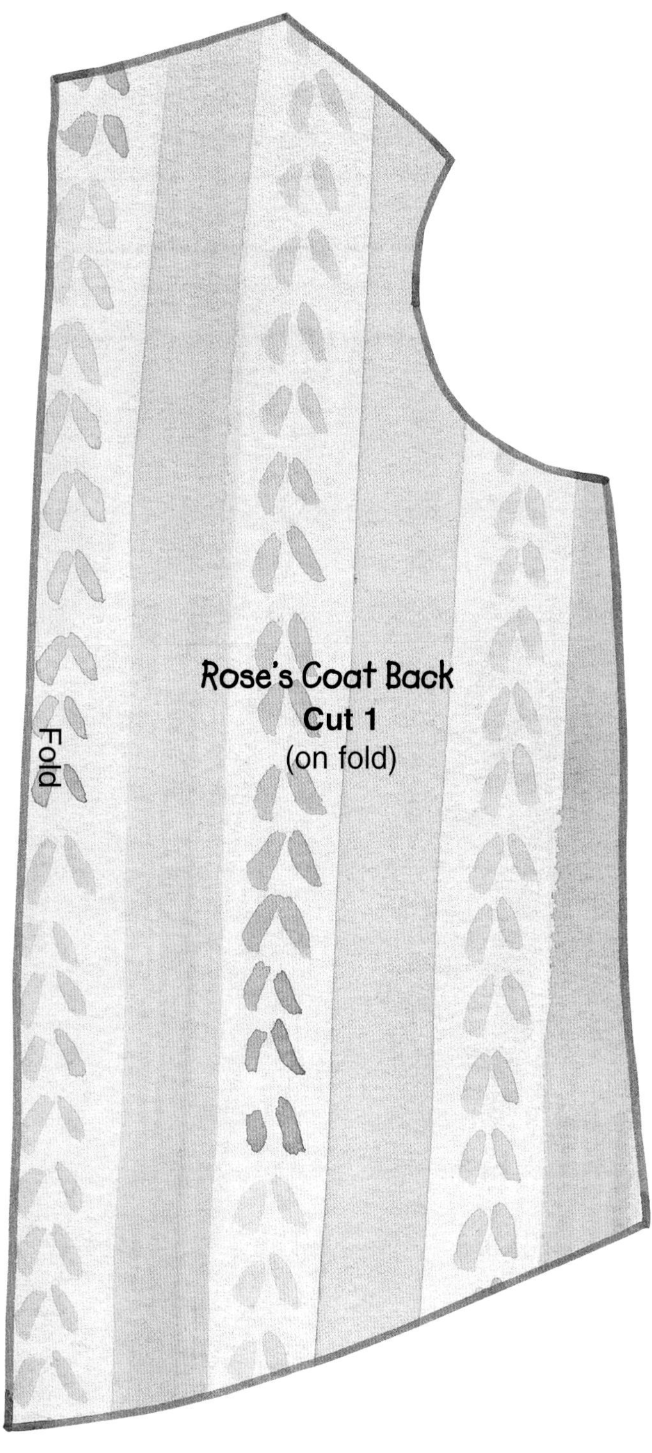

Rose likes to wear her plaid skirt and blue blazer as she addresses invitations to her prep school reunion.

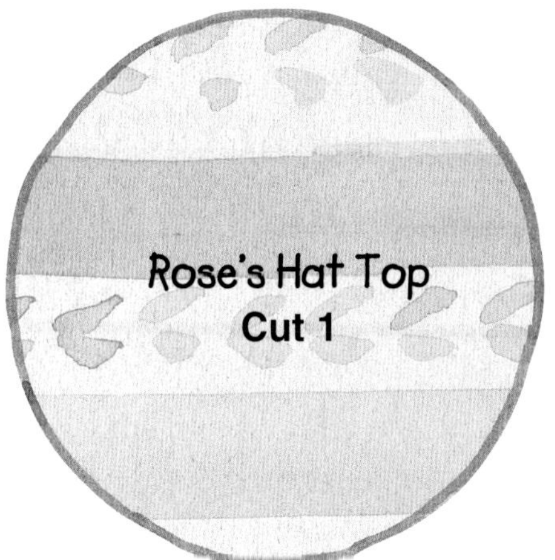

Rose in a different version of finishing details and fabrics (Her coat has a fringed lapel and no lining. Buttons have been added. Button placement for coat can be seen on page 68.)

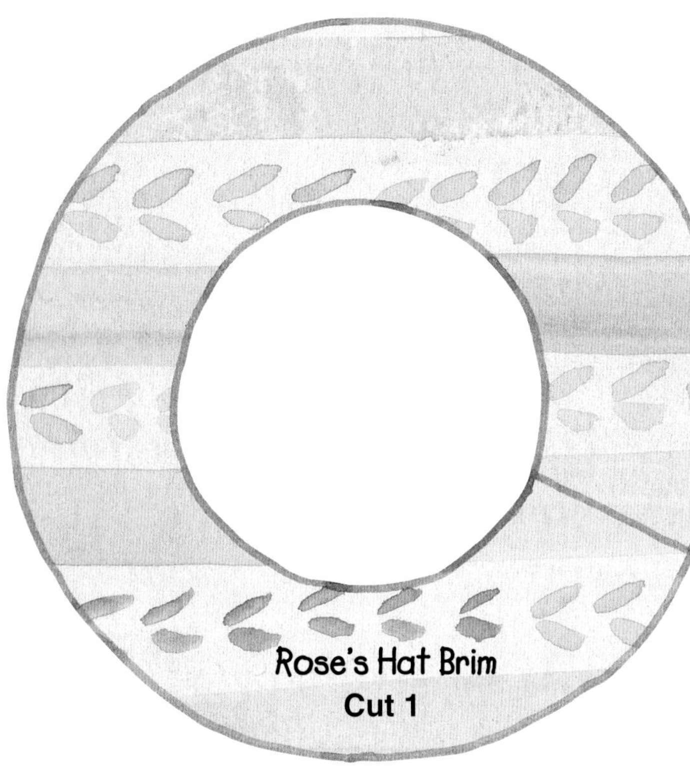

Cut along line for opening

Rose's Hat Band
Cut 1

Miss Daisey and Rose, sharing stories (Instructions for Miss Daisey, see page 122.)

Bucko is a jointed bear, except his head, which is sewn on to save assembly time. His arms and legs are jointed like a doll, with thread and buttons. He has a wonderful coat made from an old antique blanket. I designed a horse for him. You may find one in a toy store.

Materials

Buttons: medium (4); antique or wood, small (2)
Embroidery floss: brown
Eyes: glass or safety, 8 mm, black
Fabrics: felt or old blanket ($\frac{1}{4}$ yd.) for jacket; felt square (scrap) for nose; mohair or synthetic fur ($\frac{1}{4}$ yd.) for arms, ears, body, head, and legs
Plastic pellets: (1 cup)
Polyester stuffing: small bag
Ribbon: coordinating color of choice, width of choice, ($\frac{1}{2}$ yd.)
Thread: heavy; sewing, coordinating color of choice

Tools

Cardboard
Fabric marker
Measuring tape
Needles: doll, 5" or longer; embroidery; sewing
Pencil
Pins
Scissors: craft; fabric
Sewing machine with thread
Stuffing stick
Tracing paper

All seams allowances are $\frac{1}{8}$".

Beginnings

1. Read "Bear Necessities" on pages 8–17 before beginning. Organize all materials and tools needed for this project.

2. Using pencil, tracing paper, cardboard, and craft scissors, make templates of pattern pieces on pages 74–77.

3. Place templates on backs of fabric. Using fabric marker, trace patterns. Using fabric scissors, cut out fabric pieces.

4. Using sewing machine, sew darts in head. Sew head pieces, with right sides together, from front top of chin to front bottom of neck. Place gusset,

centering nose end at top of chin seam. Using pins, pin in place. Sew along one side from nose end, over top of head, to back bottom of neck. Repeat for other side.

5. Sew ear and arm pieces,with right sides together, leaving open where marked.

6. Fold leg pieces over, with right sides together. Sew around pieces, leaving open where marked.

7. Sew body darts. Sew body pieces, with right sides together, leaving open where marked. Check all seams. Turn all sewn pieces right side out.

Note: If using glass eyes, stuff head first. If using safety eyes, insert eyes first and then stuff head.

8. Using stuffing stick, stuff head firmly with polyester stuffing. Stuff arms and legs. Fill bottom of body with plastic pellets, then stuff body firmly to the top with polyester stuffing.

Face

9. Using pins, mark eye placement. Using doll needle, insert eyes onto face with heavy thread.

10. Using pins, attach ears onto head where marked on pattern. See "Ladder Stitch" on page 15. Using embroidery needle, sew ears onto head with heavy thread and Ladder Stitch.

11. Using pencil, trace desired nose pattern from page 14 onto tracing paper, creating template. Using craft scissors, cut out template. Using fabric marker, trace template onto felt. Using fabric scissors, cut out felt nose. Pin felt nose onto face.

12. See "Satin Stitch" on page 15. Using embroidery needle, embroider over felt nose with embroidery floss and Satin Stitch. Embroider mouth.

Arms, Body, & Legs

13. Using embroidery needle, gather-stitch around opening on body with heavy thread, leaving slightly open to fit base of head. Sew arms and legs closed.

14. Using doll needle, sew arms and legs onto body with heavy thread and buttons.

15. Align center seams of head and body. See "Ladder Stitch" on page 15. Using Ladder Stitch, sew head onto body with heavy thread, turning while stitching. Sew around neck twice for strength.

Jacket

16. Using sewing machine, sew shoulder seams, with right sides together, on jacket. Ease sleeves into sleeve openings, pin, and sew.

Continued on page 77.

Ear Placement

Bucko's Head
Cut 2
(one reverse)

Open

Open

Bucko stands 12" tall.

Bucko's Ear
Cut 4
(two reverse)

Open

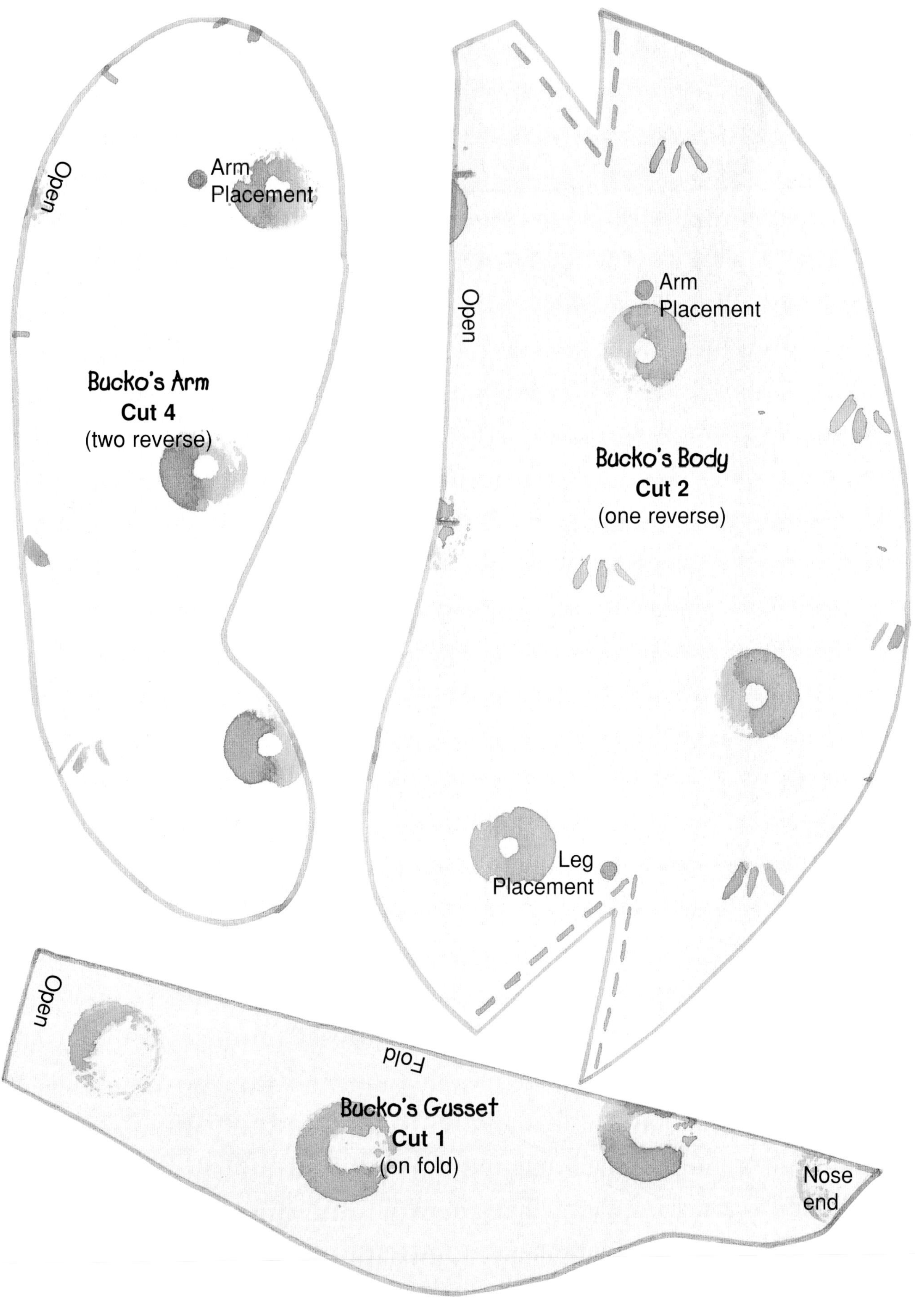
Open
Arm
Placement
Bucko's Arm
Cut 4
(two reverse)
Open
Arm
Placement
Bucko's Body
Cut 2
(one reverse)
Leg
Placement
Open
Fold
Bucko's Gusset
Cut 1
(on fold)
Nose
end

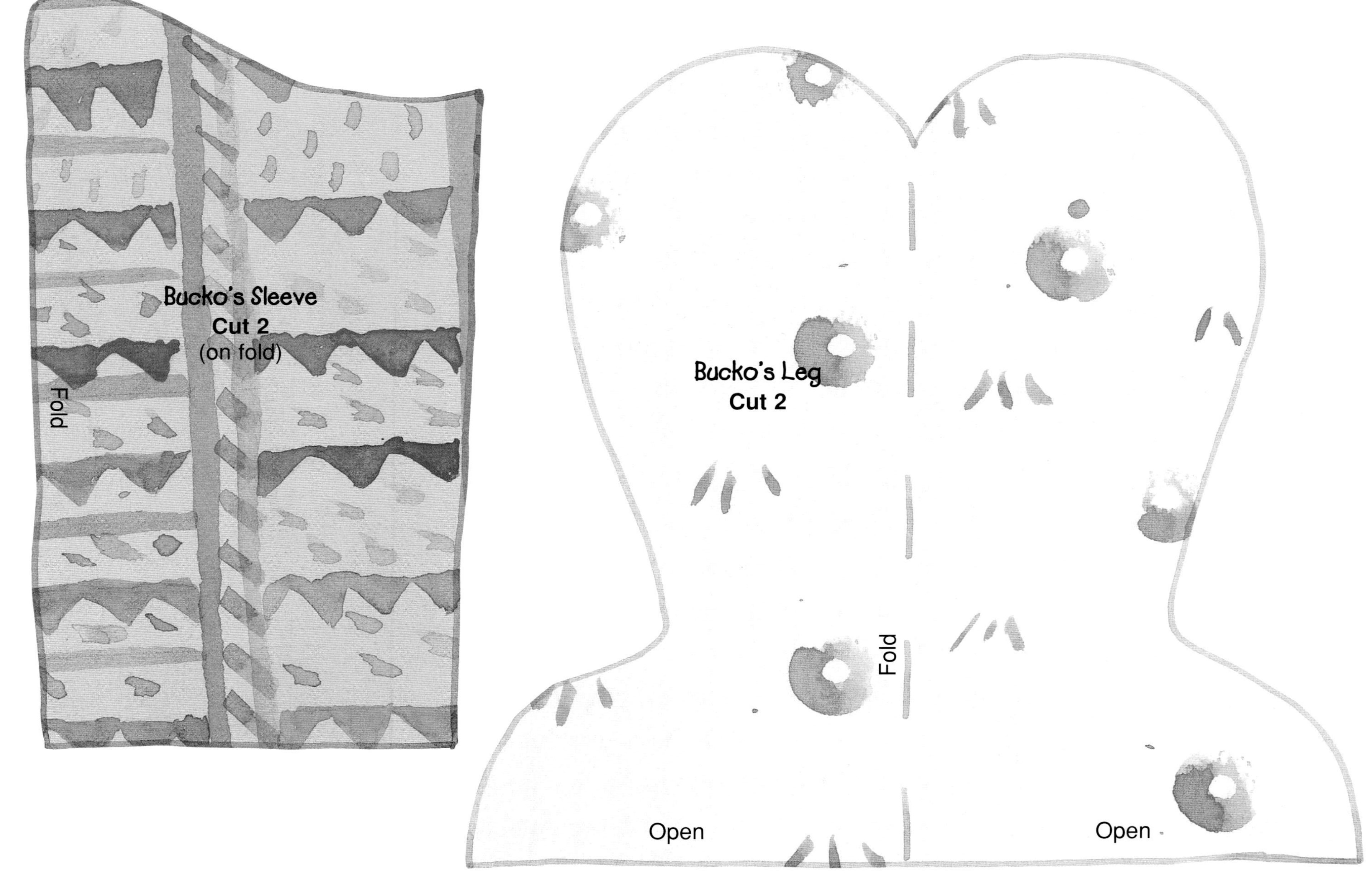
Bucko's Sleeve
Cut 2
(on fold)
Fold
Bucko's Leg
Cut 2
Fold
Open
Open

Continued from page 74.

17. Sew jacket closed from wrist on sleeve to bottom of jacket on each side. See "Blanket Stitch" on page 15. Trim hem and edges with Blanket Stitch.

18. Place jacket on bear and fold lapel back.

19. Using sewing needle, tack jacket closed with sewing thread. Sew wood or antique buttons at tack.

Finishings

20. Tie ribbon around neck for tie.

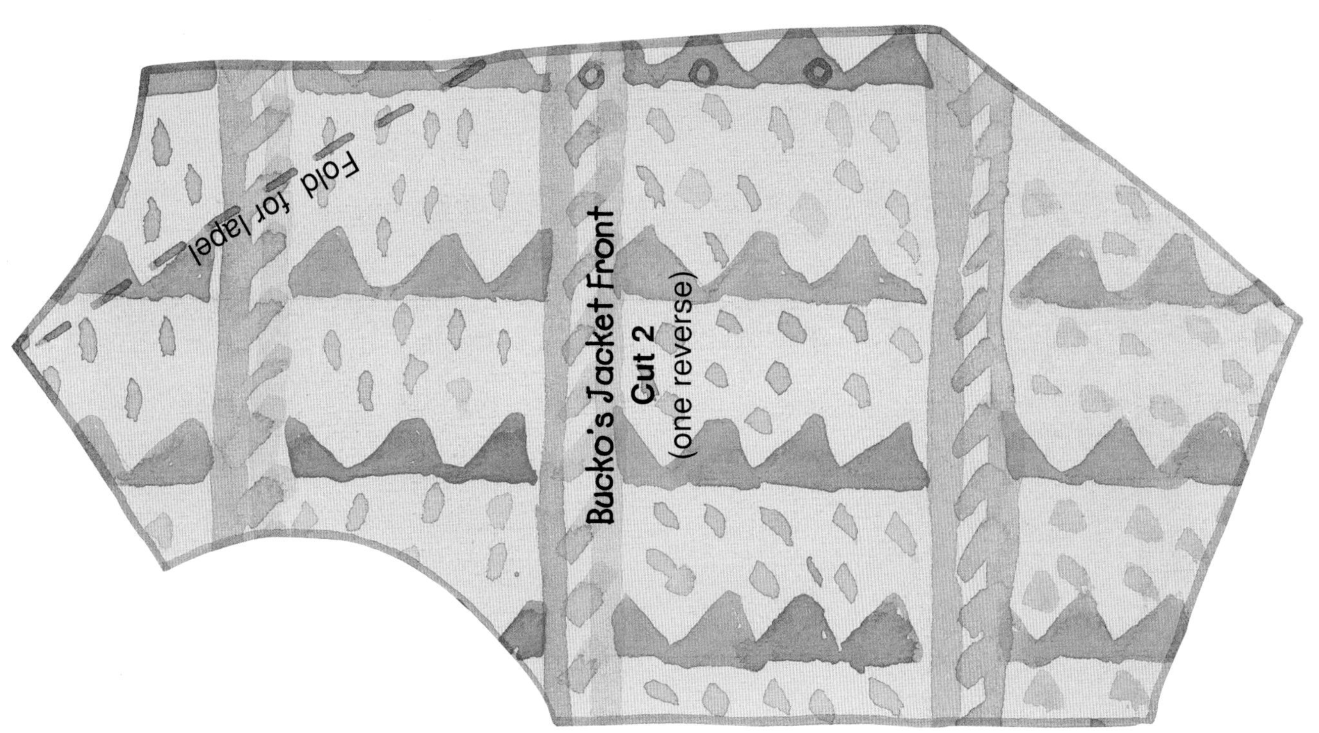

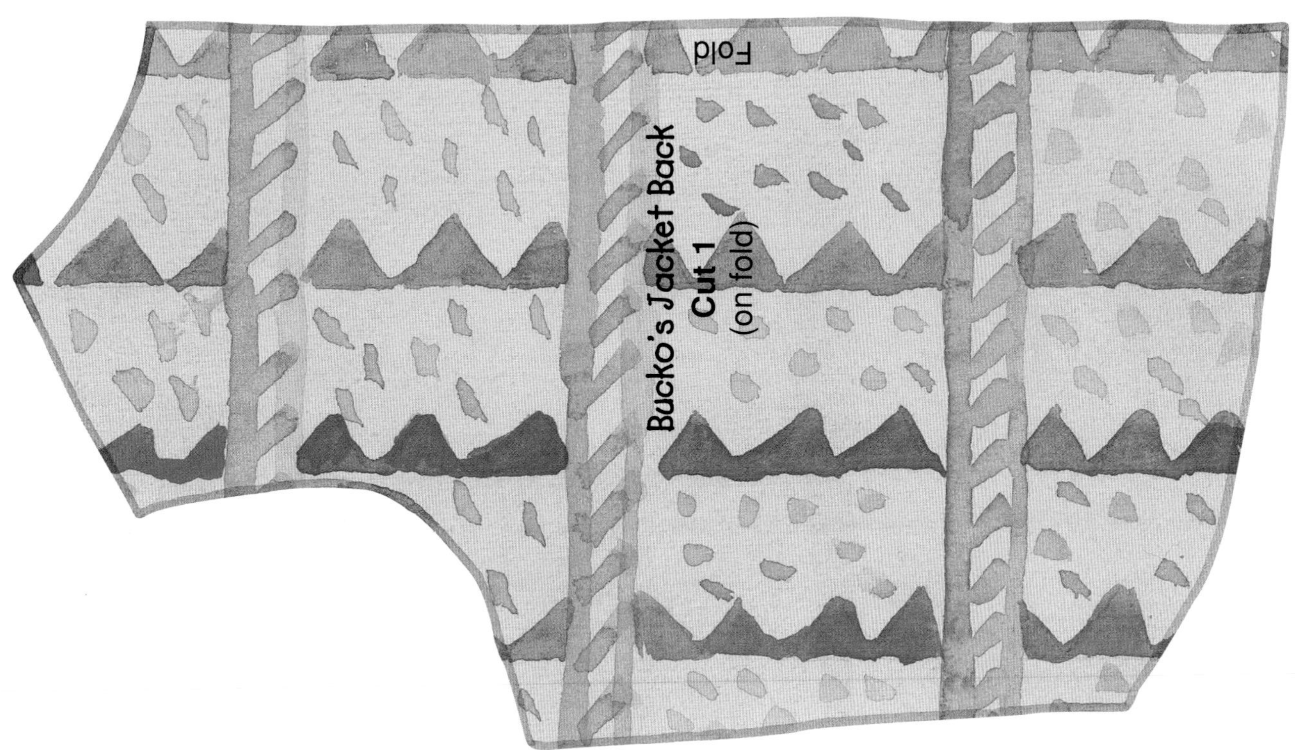

Bucko, waitin' for his lemonade

Joshua Bunny came to me after reading the story of Benjamin Bunny by Beatrice Potter. I have always loved the world of Beatrice Potter and Brambley Hedge and the attitude of the characters in this book surely reflect this. Joshua has a cut-a-way coat made of felt, flannel, or wool. Joshua Bunny has plastic pellets in his belly so that he sits nicely. You can add a bow tie for a more formal occasion, like Joshua's friend on the left on page 79.

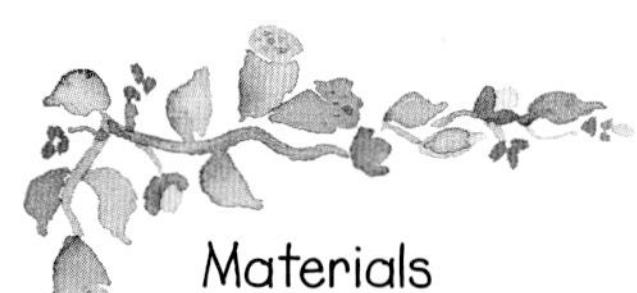

Materials

Buttons: medium (4); small (3)
Embroidery floss: brown
Eyes: glass or safety, 10 mm, black
Fabrics: felt, wool, or blanket (1/4 yd.) for coat; felt square (scrap) for nose; printed or striped (1/8 yd.) for bow tie; synthetic fur or mohair, (1/4 yd.) for arms, ears, body, head, legs, and tail
Plastic pellets: (3/4 cup)
Plastic vegetable or fruit: tiny
Polyester stuffing: small bag
Thread: heavy; sewing, coordinating color of choice

Tools

Cardboard
Fabric marker
Iron
Measuring tape
Needles: doll, 5" or longer; embroidery; sewing
Pencil
Pins
Scissors: craft; fabric
Sewing machine with thread
Stuffing stick
Tracing paper

All seam allowances are 1/8".

Beginnings

1. Read "Bear Necessities" on pages 8-17 before beginning. Organize all materials and tools needed for this project.

2. Using pencil, tracing paper, cardboard, and craft scissors, make templates of pattern pieces on pages 81-83.

3. Place templates on backs of fabric. Using fabric marker, trace pattern. Using fabric scissors, cut out fabric pieces.

4. Using sewing machine, sew darts in head.

5. Sew head, ear, arm, and leg pieces, with right sides together, leaving open where marked.

6. Gather-stitch around tail.

7. Sew body pieces, with center seams first. Sew sides and bottoms, with right sides together, leaving open where marked. Check all seams. Turn all sewn pieces right side out.

Note: If using glass eyes, stuff head first. If using safety eyes, insert eyes first and then stuff head.

8. Using stuffing stick, stuff head firmly with polyester stuffing. Stuff arms, legs, and tail. Fill bottom of body with plastic pellets, then stuff body firmly to the top with polyester stuffing.

Face

9. Using pins, mark eye placement. Using doll needle, insert eyes onto face with heavy thread.

10. Using pins, attach ears onto head where marked on pattern. See "Ladder Stitch" on page 15. Using embroidery needle, sew ears onto head with heavy thread and Ladder Stitch.

11. Using pencil, trace desired nose pattern from page 14 onto tracing paper, creating template. Using craft scissors, cut out template. Using fabric marker, trace template onto felt. Using fabric scissors, cut out felt nose. Pin felt nose onto face.

Joshua stands 10" high.

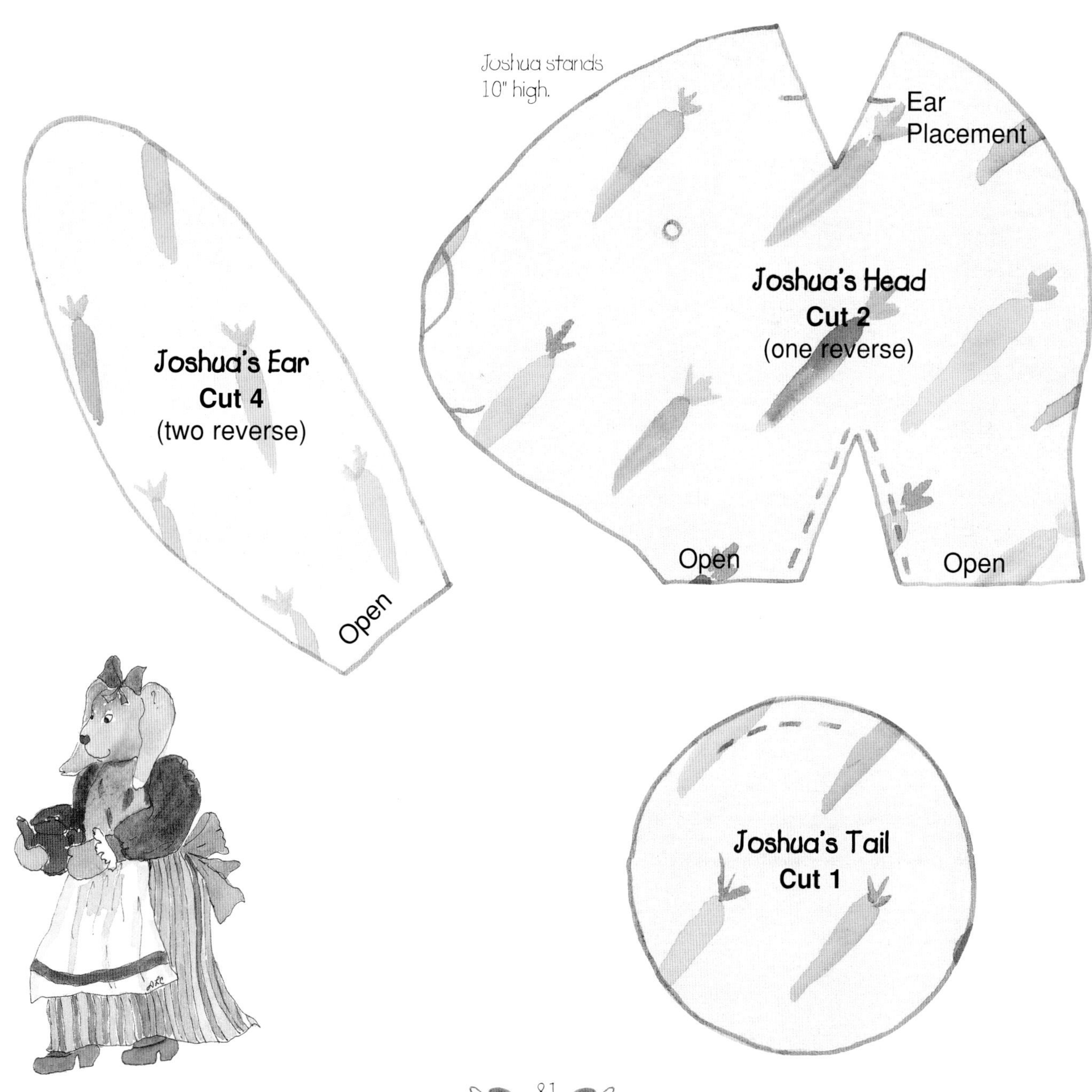

12. See "Satin Stitch" on page 15. Using embroidery needle, embroider over felt nose with embroidery floss and Satin Stitch. Embroider mouth.

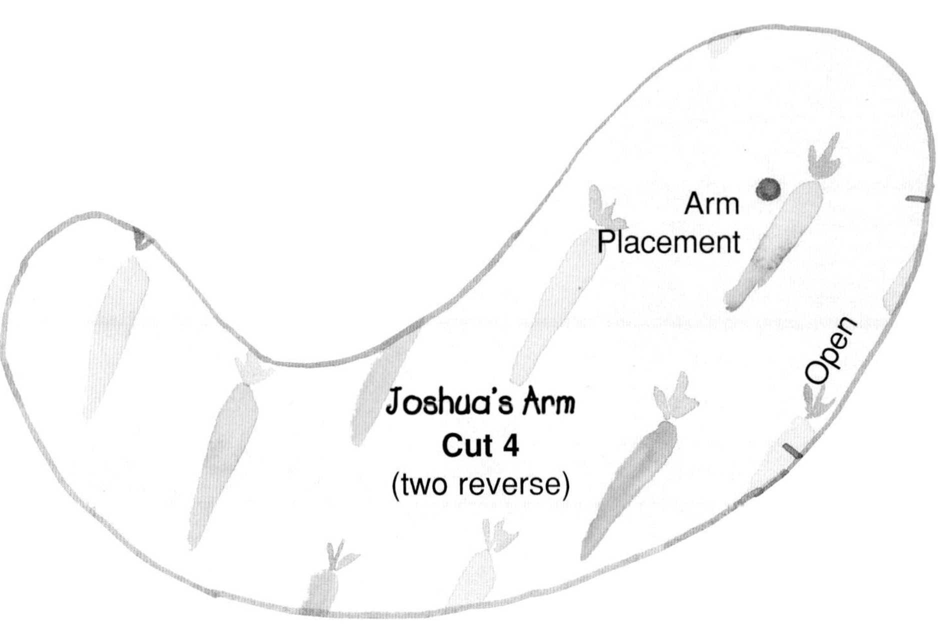

Arms, Legs, Body, & Tail

13. Using embroidery needle, gather-stitch around opening on body with heavy thread, leaving slightly open to fit base of head. Sew arms and legs closed.

14. Using doll needle, sew arms and legs onto body with heavy thread and buttons.

15. Align center seams of head and body. See "Ladder Stitch" on page 15. Using embroidery needle, sew head onto body with heavy thread and Ladder Stitch. Sew around head twice for strength.

16. Pull gathering threads on tail to close. See 'Ladder Stitch" on page 15. Sew tail onto back of bunny with embroidery floss and Ladder Stitch.

See completed bunny on page 84 before adding clothing.

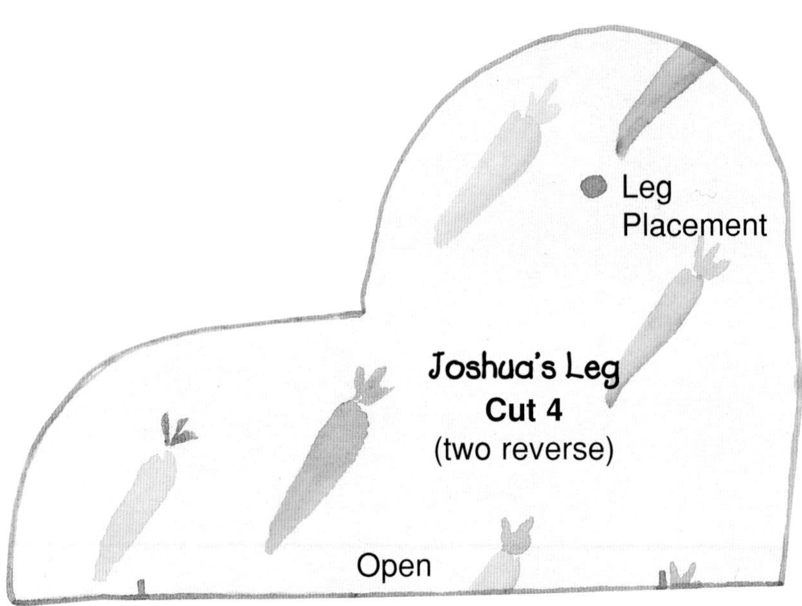

Coat

17. See "Bucko's Jacket" on pages 76-77. Using fabric marker, trace pattern pieces for Bucko's jacket onto felt, flannel, or wool fabric. Using fabric scissors, cut out fabric pieces.

18. Using sewing machine, sew shoulder seams, with right sides together, on coat. Ease sleeves into sleeve openings, pin, and sew.

19. Sew coat closed from wrist on sleeve to bottom of coat on each side. See "Blanket Stitch" on page 15. Trim hem and edges with Blanket Stitch.

> **Tip:**
> Try sewing pipe cleaners inside ears, so that they can bend in different directions.

20. Using sewing needle, sew buttons on coat edge with sewing thread.

21. Place coat on bunny.

Bow Tie

22. Using fabric scissors, cut 2" x 4" piece of scrap fabric.

23. Using iron, press 1/4" folds on 4" sides of cut fabric.

24. Fold ends to center, overlapping 1/4". Using sewing needle, sew in place.

25. Using fabric scissors, cut 1 1/2" x 2" piece of scrap fabric.

26. Using iron, press 1/4" folds on 2" sides of cut fabric.

27. Wrap small piece of fabric around center of larger piece of fabric. Gather. Using sewing needle, sew in place with sewing thread.

28. Place bow tie on bunny's neck. Tack bow to secure with sewing thread.

Finishings

29. Sew paws together and place plastic vegetable or fruit in paws.

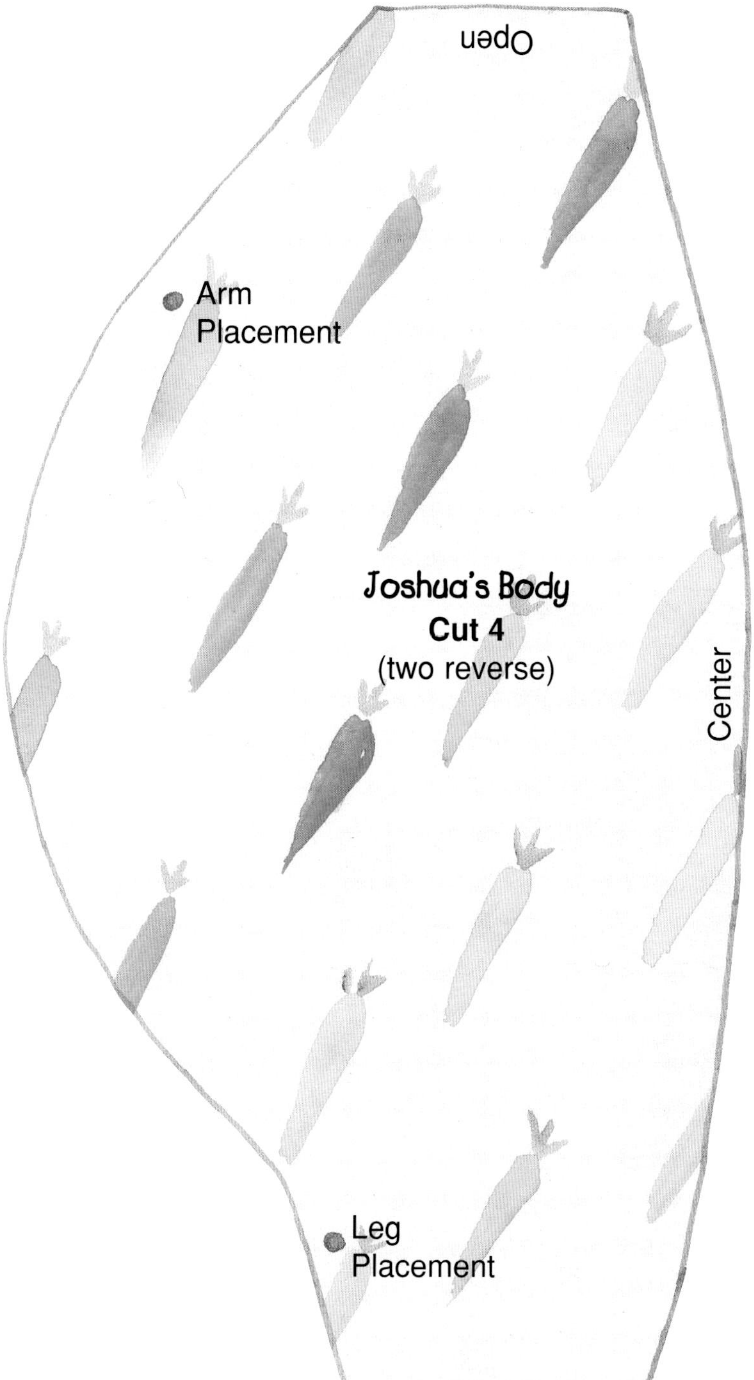

Open

Arm Placement

Joshua's Body
Cut 4
(two reverse)

Center

Leg Placement

Joshua before adding clothing

Beary Special

Miss Gabby, enjoying a quiet moment (Instructions for Miss Gabby, see page 91.)

Benjamen Bear has long legs, hiking boots, and a cute sweater. His stocking cap is made from the top of a sock. I have filled his bottom with some plastic pellets, so that he sits nicely on a shelf with his legs crossed or hanging down. I like to take my bear shopping for his socks and shoes. He will always make a great hit!

Materials

Buttons: medium (2)
Embroidery floss: brown
Eyes: glass or safety, 8 mm, black
Fabrics: felt or quilted batting (1/4 yd.) for arms, ears, and head; felt square (scrap) for nose; flannel (1/3 yd.) for body and legs, (1/2 yd) for scarf
Hiking boots: child's size 2
Plastic pellets: (1 cup)
Polyester stuffing: small bag
Shoelaces: red
Socks
Sweater: small baby or medium teddy bear
Thread: heavy; sewing, coordinating color of choice

Tools

Cardboard
Fabric marker
Needles: doll, 5" or longer; embroidery; sewing
Pencil
Pins
Scissors: craft; scissors
Sewing machine with thread
Stuffing stick
Tracing Paper

All seam allowances are 1/8".

Beginnings

1. Read "Bear Necessities" on pages 8-17 before beginning. Organize all materials and tools needed for this project.

2. Using pencil, tracing paper, cardboard, and craft scissors, make templates of pattern pieces on page 88-90.

3. Place templates onto backs of fabric. Using fabric marker, trace pattern. Using fabric scissors, cut out fabric pieces.

4. Using sewing machine, sew darts in head.

5. Sew head, ear, and arm pieces, with right sides together, leaving open where marked.

6. Sew body pieces, with center seams first. Sew sides, with right sides together, leaving open where marked. Match seams, then sew across bottom. Check all seams. Turn all sewn pieces right side out.

Note: If using glass eyes, stuff head first. If using safety eyes, insert eyes first and then stuff head.

7. Using stuffing stick, stuff head firmly with polyester stuffing. Stuff arms. Fill bottom of body with plastic pellets, then stuff body firmly to the top with polyester stuffing.

8. See "Ladder Stitch" on page 15. Using embroidery needle, sew head and body closed with embroidery floss and Ladder Stitch.

Face

9. Using pins, mark eye placement. Using doll needle, pull eyes onto face with heavy thread.

10. Using pins, attach ears onto head where marked on pattern. See "Ladder Stitch" on page 15. Using embroidery needle, sew

Benjamen's Ear
Cut 4
(two reverse)
Open

Benjamen stands 20" tall.

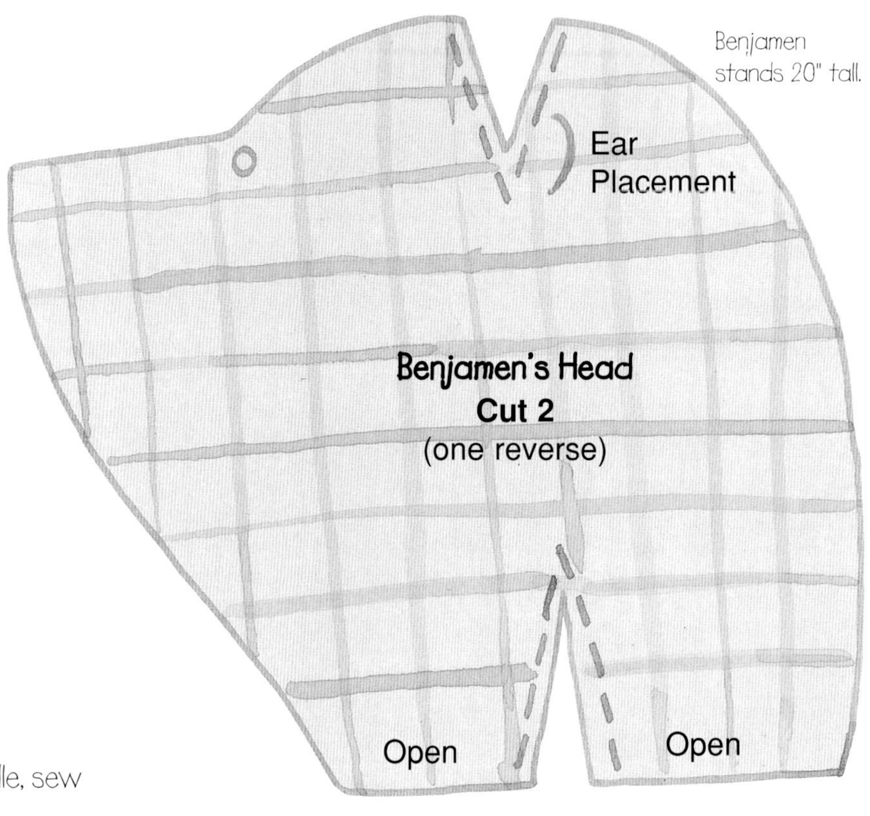

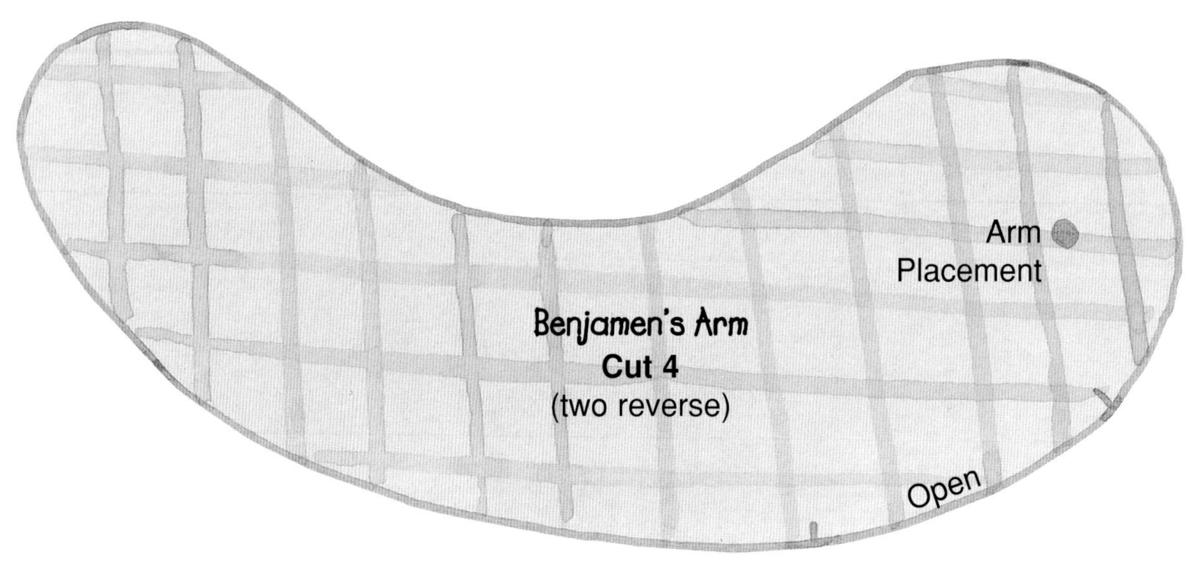

ears onto head with heavy thread and Ladder Stitch.

11. Using pencil, trace desired nose pattern from page 14 onto tracing paper, creating template. Using craft scissors, cut out template. Using fabric marker, trace template onto felt. Using fabric scissors, cut out felt nose. Pin felt nose onto face.

12. See "Satin Stitch" on page 15. Using embroidery needle, embroider over felt nose with embroidery floss and Satin Stitch. Embroider mouth.

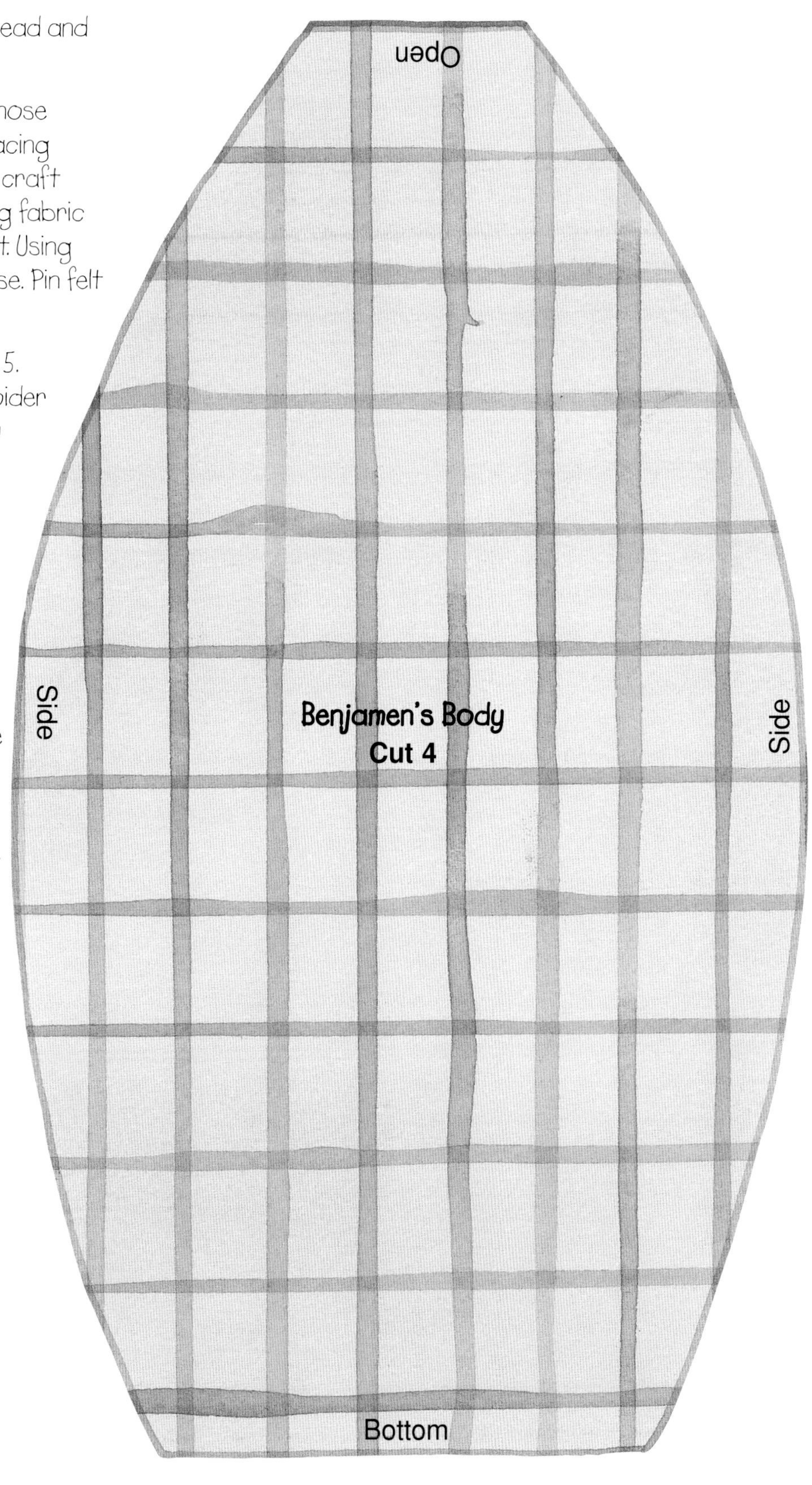

Arms, Body, & Legs

13. Using embroidery needle, gather-stitch around opening on body with heavy thread, leaving slightly open to fit base of head. Sew arms closed.

14. Using doll needle, sew arms onto body $2\frac{1}{2}$" from neck edge with heavy thread and buttons.

15. Using stuffing stick, stuff legs to first mark with polyester stuffing. Match seams. Using sewing machine, sew across legs. Feet will be facing forward. Repeat process for second mark.

16. Using stuffing stick, stuff legs 2" from top. Using sewing machine, sew across legs, leaving unstuffed section for hem.

17. Fold in hem to insides of legs. Sew legs onto bottom of body.

18. Align center seams of head and body. See "Ladder Stitch" on page 15. Using embroidery needle, sew head onto body with heavy thread and Ladder Stitch. Sew around neck twice for strength.

Scarf

19. Using fabric scissors, cut 3" x 18" piece of flannel fabric.

20. Using sewing needle, pull threads out along all edges to create fringe.

21. Tie scarf loosely around bear's neck.

Hat

22. Using fabric scissors, cut "hat" from old sock along dotted line. See Diagram A.

Diagram A

23. Using sewing needle, sew raw edges together with sewing thread, closing top of hat. Fold bottom edge up for brim.

24. Place hat on bear's head and tack to secure with sewing thread.

Attach pattern to top of pattern on left with transparent tape before tracing and cutting fabric.

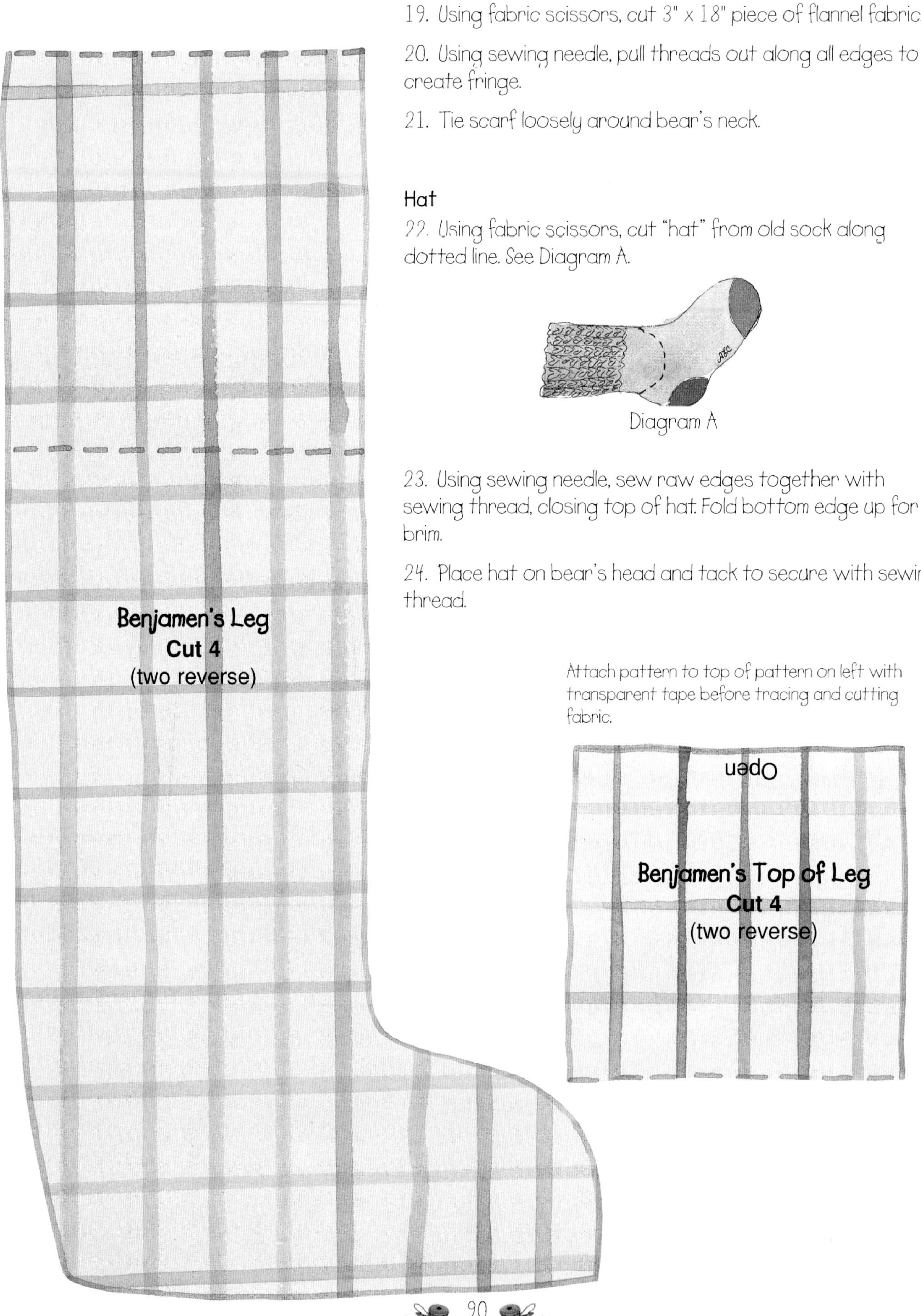

Miss Gabby

Miss Gabby is a fat bear with long legs that hang from her chair in a life-like manner. Her body is weighted with plastic pellets so she can sit perfectly. She is made of quilted batting; however, she can be sewn from felt or synthetic fur, if desired.

Materials

Buttons: medium (2)
Embroidery floss: brown
Eyes: glass or safety, 8 mm, black
Fabrics: felt square, peach, black (scraps) for nose and shoes; flannel (3/4 yd.) for body and dress; gingham (1/4 yd.) for heart and scarf; low-loft quilt batting, felt, or fur (1/3 yd.) for arms, ears, head, and legs
Lace: 1/2"-1"-wide (1 yd.); eyelet, 6"-wide (12")
Plastic pellets: (1 cup)
Polyester stuffing: small bag
Rick rack: white (1 pkg.)
Snaps: small (2)
Thread: heavy; sewing, coordinating color of choice

Tools

Cardboard
Fabric marker
Needles: doll, 5" or longer; embroidery; sewing
Pencil
Pins
Scissors: craft; fabric
Sewing machine with thread
Stuffing stick
Tracing paper

All seam allowances are 1/8".

Beginnings

1. Read "Bear Necessities" on pages 8-17 before beginning. Organize all materials and tools needed for this project.

2. Using sewing machine, sew black felt onto bottom of leg fabric. See Diagram A on facing page.

3. Using pencil, tracing paper, cardboard, and craft scissors, make templates of pattern pieces on pages 93–97.

4. Place templates on backs of fabric. Using fabric marker, trace pattern. Trace leg pattern with shoe portion placed on black felt. See Diagram A. Using fabric scissors, cut out fabric pieces.

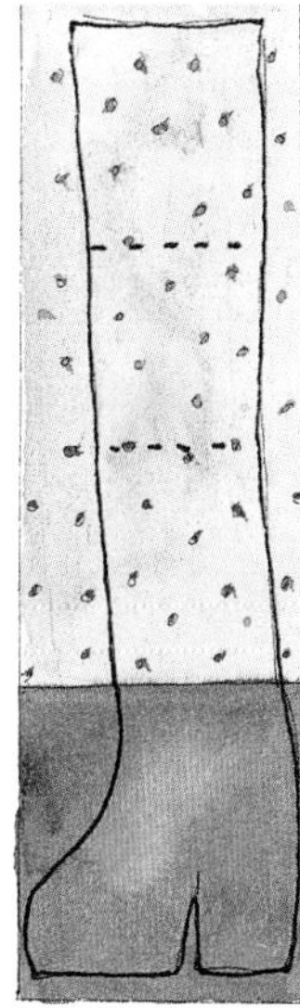
Diagram A

5. Using sewing machine, sew head, ear, arm, and heart pieces, with right sides together, leaving open where marked.

6. Sew body pieces, with center seams first. Sew sides and bottoms, with right sides together, leaving open where marked. Check all seams. Turn all sewn pieces right side out

Note: If using glass eyes, stuff head first. If using safety eyes, insert eyes first and then stuff head.

7. Using stuffing stick, stuff head firmly with polyester stuffing. Stuff arms and heart. Fill bottom of body with plastic pellets, then stuff body firmly to the top with polyester stuffing.

8. See "Ladder Stitch" on page 15. Using embroidery needle, sew head and body closed with heavy thread, and Ladder Stitch.

Face

9. Using pins, mark eye placement. Using doll needle, pull eyes onto face.

10. Using pins, attach ears onto head where marked on pattern. See "Ladder Stitch" on page 15. Using embroidery needle, sew ears onto head with heavy thread and Ladder Stitch.

11. Using pencil, trace desired nose pattern from page 14 onto tracing paper, creating template. Using craft scissors, cut out template. Using fabric marker, trace template onto felt. Using fabric scissors, cut out felt nose. Pin felt nose onto face.

12. See "Satin Stitch" on page 15. Using embroidery needle, embroider over felt nose with embroidery floss and Satin Stitch. Embroider mouth.

Miss Gabby stands 18" tall.

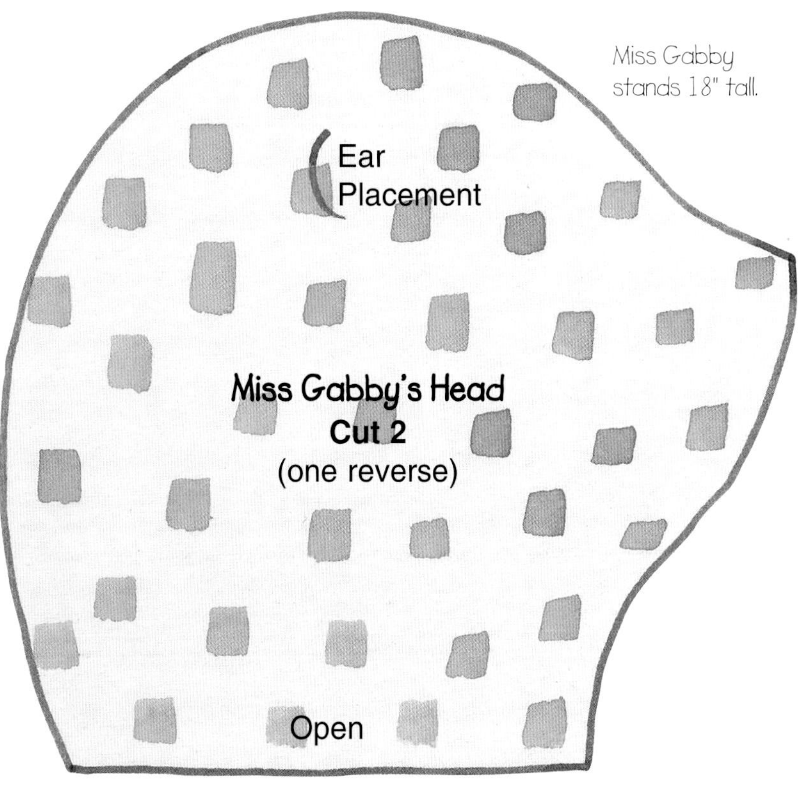

Arms, Body ,& Legs

13. Using embroidery needle, gather-stitch around opening on body with heavy thread, leaving slightly open to fit base of head. Sew arms closed.

14. Using doll needle, sew arms onto body with heavy thread and buttons.

15. Align center seams of head and body. See "Ladder Stitch" on page 15. Using embroidery needle, sew head onto body with heavy thread and Ladder Stitch. Sew around neck twice for strength.

16. Using stuffing stick, stuff legs to first mark with polyester stuffing. Match seams. Using sewing machine, sew across legs. Feet will be facing forward. Repeat process for second mark.

17. Using stuffing stick, stuff legs 2" from top. Using sewing machine, sew across legs, leaving unstuffed section for hem.

18. Fold in hem to insides of legs. Sew legs onto bottom of body. See Diagram B at right.

Shoes

19. Create shoe laces with embroidery floss.

Diagram B

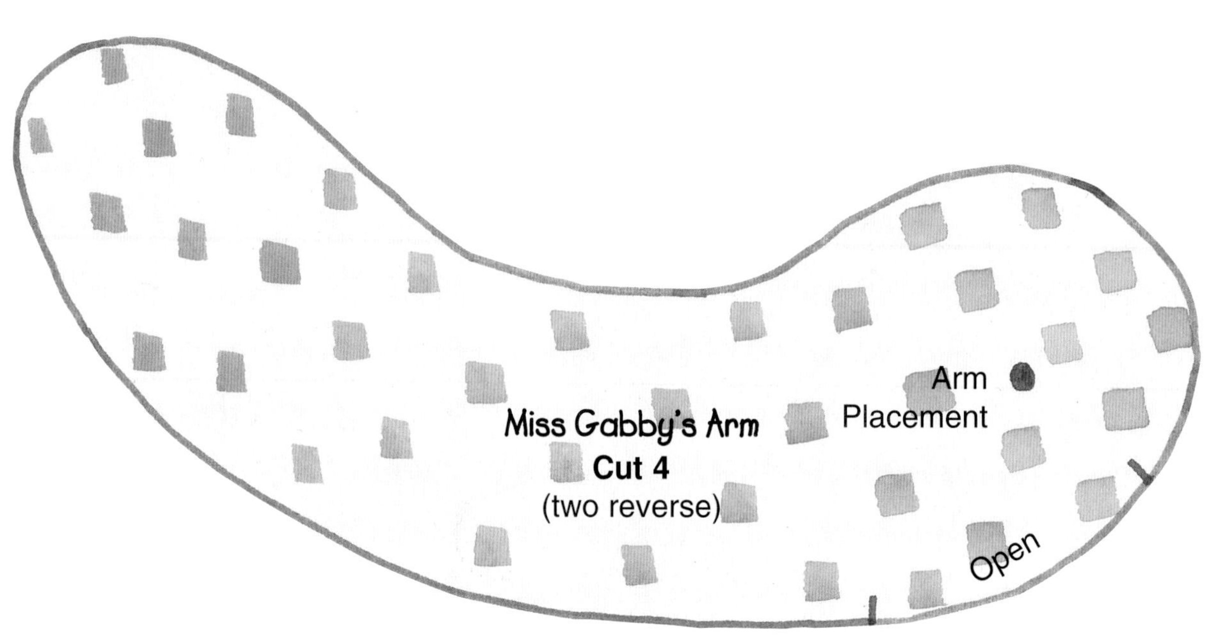

Dress

20. Using fabric scissors, cut 12" x 33" piece of flannel for skirt.

21. Using sewing machine, sew rick rack onto bottom of skirt.

22. Gather-stitch top long edge of skirt.

23. Sew shoulder seams, with right sides together, on bodice. Turn down neck edge 1/4" and hem.

24. Gather-stitch top and bottom of sleeves, fitting sleeves to bear's arms.

25. Sew lace trim at end of sleeves. Ease sleeves into sleeve openings, pin, and sew.

26. Sew bodice closed from wrist on sleeve to bottom of bodice on each side.

27. Sew gathered skirt to bodice.

28. Hem dress 2" on skirt bottom.

29. Sew up back seam, leaving open 1" below waist. Fold edge of opening in 1/4" and sew.

30. Sew lace trim onto neck edge.

31. Using sewing needle, sew snaps along edge with sewing thread.

Pantaloons

32. Using fabric scissors, cut two lengths of eyelet lace from leg pattern. Using sewing machine, sew seam down each piece, with right sides together. Turn right side out.

Continued on page 97.

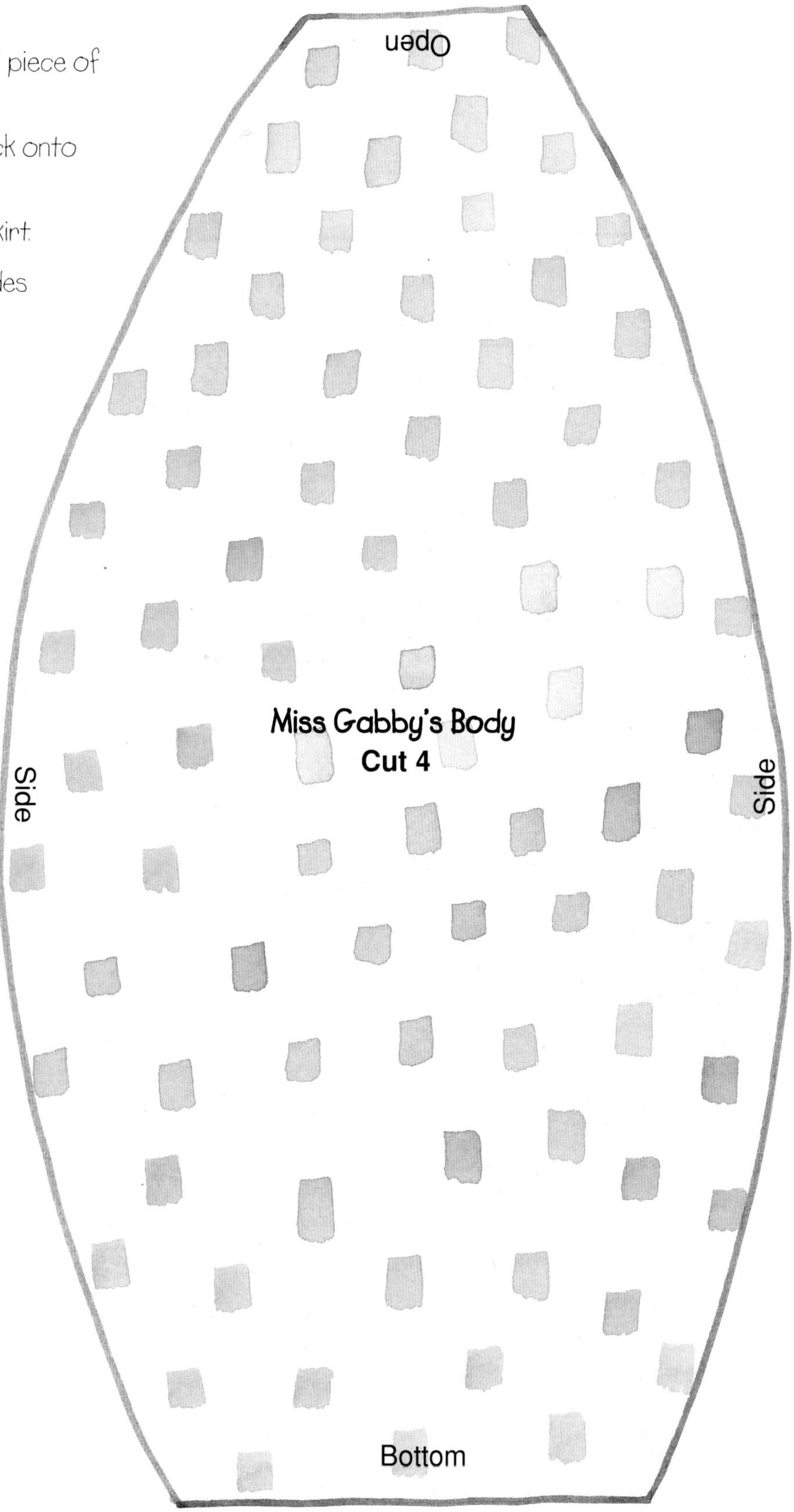

Open

Miss Gabby's Body
Cut 4

Side

Side

Bottom

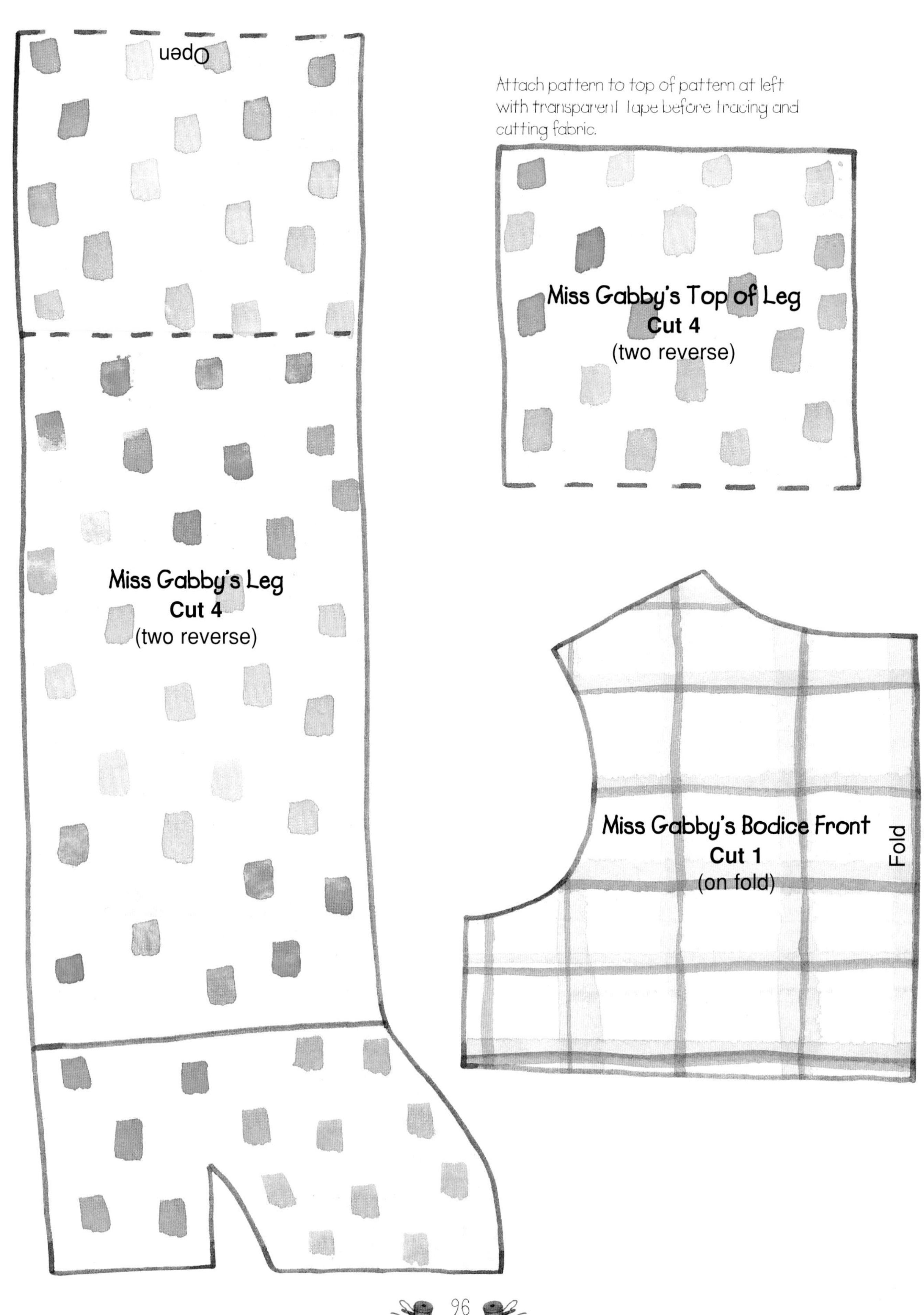
Open
Attach pattern to top of pattern at left with transparent tape before tracing and cutting fabric.
Miss Gabby's Top of Leg
Cut 4
(two reverse)
Miss Gabby's Leg
Cut 4
(two reverse)
Miss Gabby's Bodice Front
Cut 1
(on fold)
Fold

Continued from page 95.

33. Slip pantaloons over legs. Using sewing needle. sew to top of legs.

Scarf

34. Using fabric scissors, cut triangle from 15" square of fabric.

35. Tie scarf to bear's head.

Finishings

36. Using sewing needle, sew bear paws together with sewing thread. Sew heart to arm.

37. Place fruit or flowers in arms, if desired.

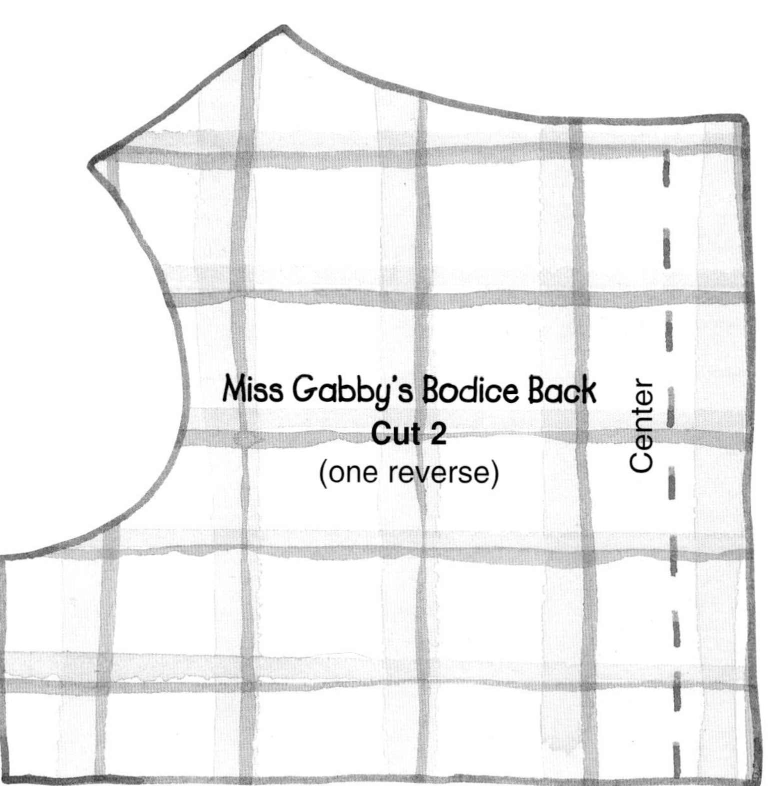

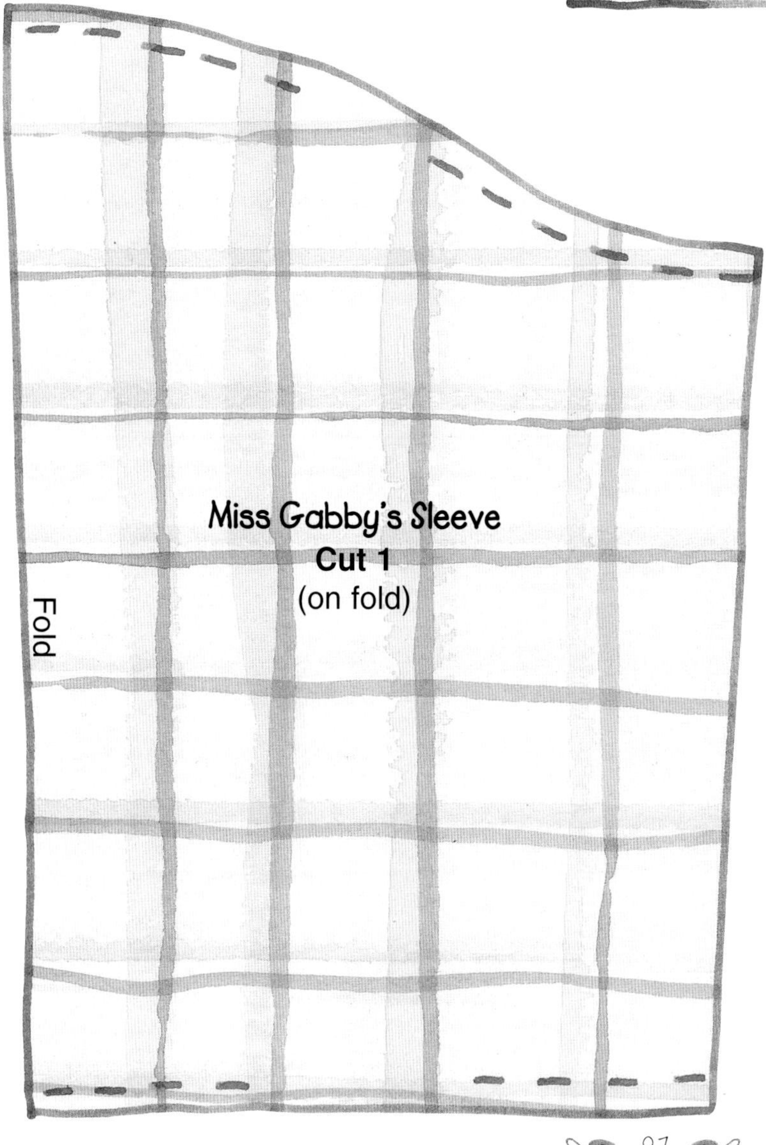

Miss Gabby and her flowers

Miss Jenny

Miss Jenny's head and body are one piece. Her skirt is weighted with plastic pellets to balance her so she will stand, having sufficient weight to hold a door open. Look through your jewelry box to find something special to add to your creation.

Materials

Brooch or decorative button
Buttons: medium (2)
Chopstick
Embroidery floss: brown
Eyes: glass or safety, 7 or 8 mm, black
Fabrics: felt square (scrap) for nose; flannel (1/3 yd.) for skirt; loose-weave (1/6 yd.) for shawl; mohair or synthetic fur (1/3 yd.) for arms, ears, head, and body
Kitchen broom
Lace trim: (1/2 yd.)
Plastic pellets: (1 cup)
Polyester stuffing: small bag
Straw hat (optional)
Thread: heavy; sewing, coordinating color of choice
Twist tie

Tools

Cardboard
Craft glue
Fabric marker
Measuring tape
Needles: doll, 5" or longer; embroidery; sewing
Pencil
Pins
Scissors: craft; fabric
Sewing machine with thread
Stuffing stick
Tracing paper
Transparent tape

All seam allowances are 1/8".

Beginnings

1. Read "Bear Necessities" on pages 8-17 before beginning. Organize all materials and tools needed for this project.

2. Using pencil, tracing paper, cardboard, and craft scissors, make templates of pattern pieces on pages 101-103.

3. Place templates on backs of fabric. Using fabric marker, trace pattern. Using fabric scissors, cut out fabric pieces.

4. Using sewing machine, sew darts in head/body.

5. Sew ear and arm pieces, with right sides together, leaving open where marked.

6. Sew head/body pieces, with right sides together, leaving open where marked. Check all seams. Turn all sewn pieces right side out.

Note: If using glass eyes, stuff head first. If using safety eyes, insert eyes first and then stuff head.

7. Using stuffing stick stuff head firmly with polyester stuffing. Stuff arms. Fill bottom of body with plastic pellets, then stuff body firmly to the top with polyester stuffing.

8. See "Ladder Stitch" on page 15. Using embroidery needle, sew head and body closed with embroidery floss and Ladder Stitch.

Face

9. Using pins, mark eye placement. Using doll needle, pull eyes onto face with heavy thread.

10. Using pins, attach ears onto head where marked on pattern. See "Ladder Stitch" on page 15. Using embroidery needle, sew ears onto head with heavy thread.

11. Using pencil, trace desired nose pattern from page 14 onto tracing paper, creating template. Using craft scissors, cut out template. Using fabric marker, trace template onto felt. Using fabric scissors, cut out felt nose. Pin felt nose onto face.

12. See "Satin Stitch" on page 15. Using embroidery needle, embroider over felt nose with embroidery floss and Satin Stitch. Embroider mouth.

Arms & Body

13. Using embroidery needle, sew arms closed.

14. Using doll needle, sew arms onto body with heavy thread and buttons.

See completed bear on page 105 before adding clothing.

Continued on page 103.

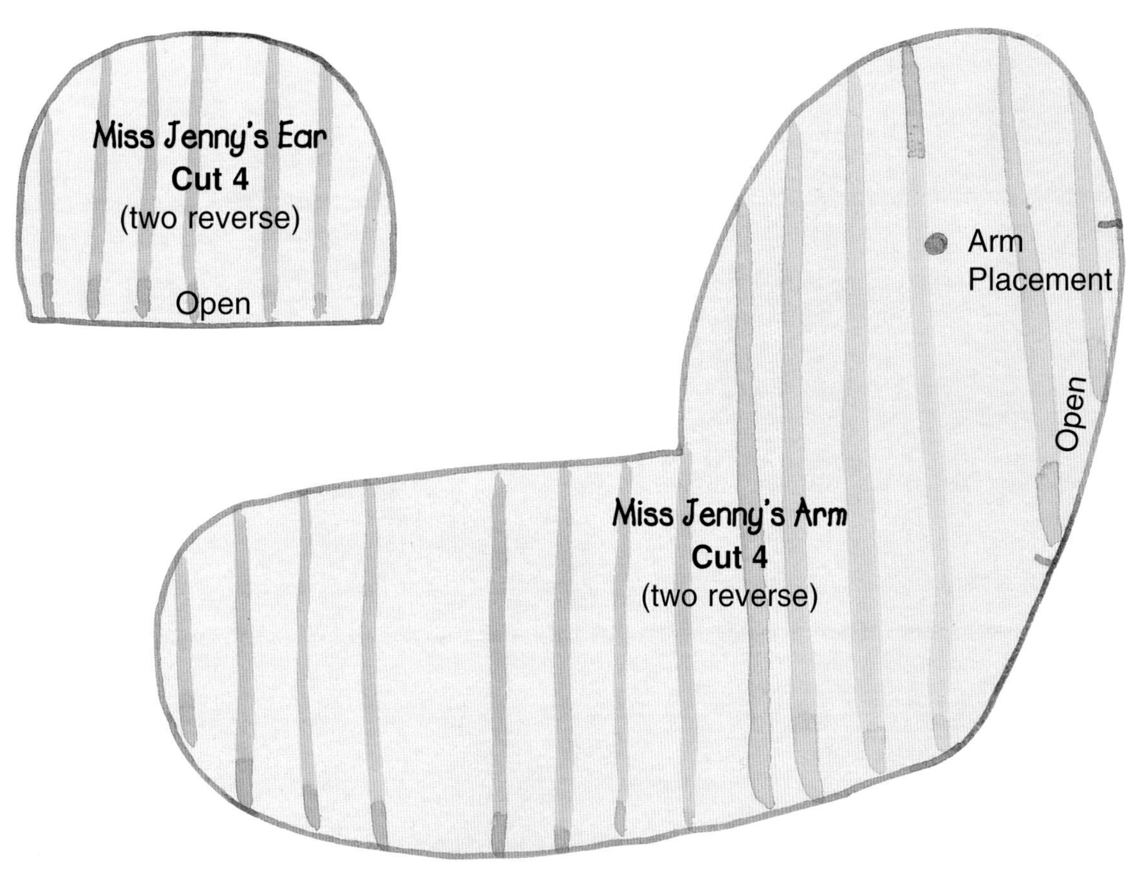

She looks somewhat like a teddy bear bowling pin! What do you think?

Miss Jenny stands 12" tall.

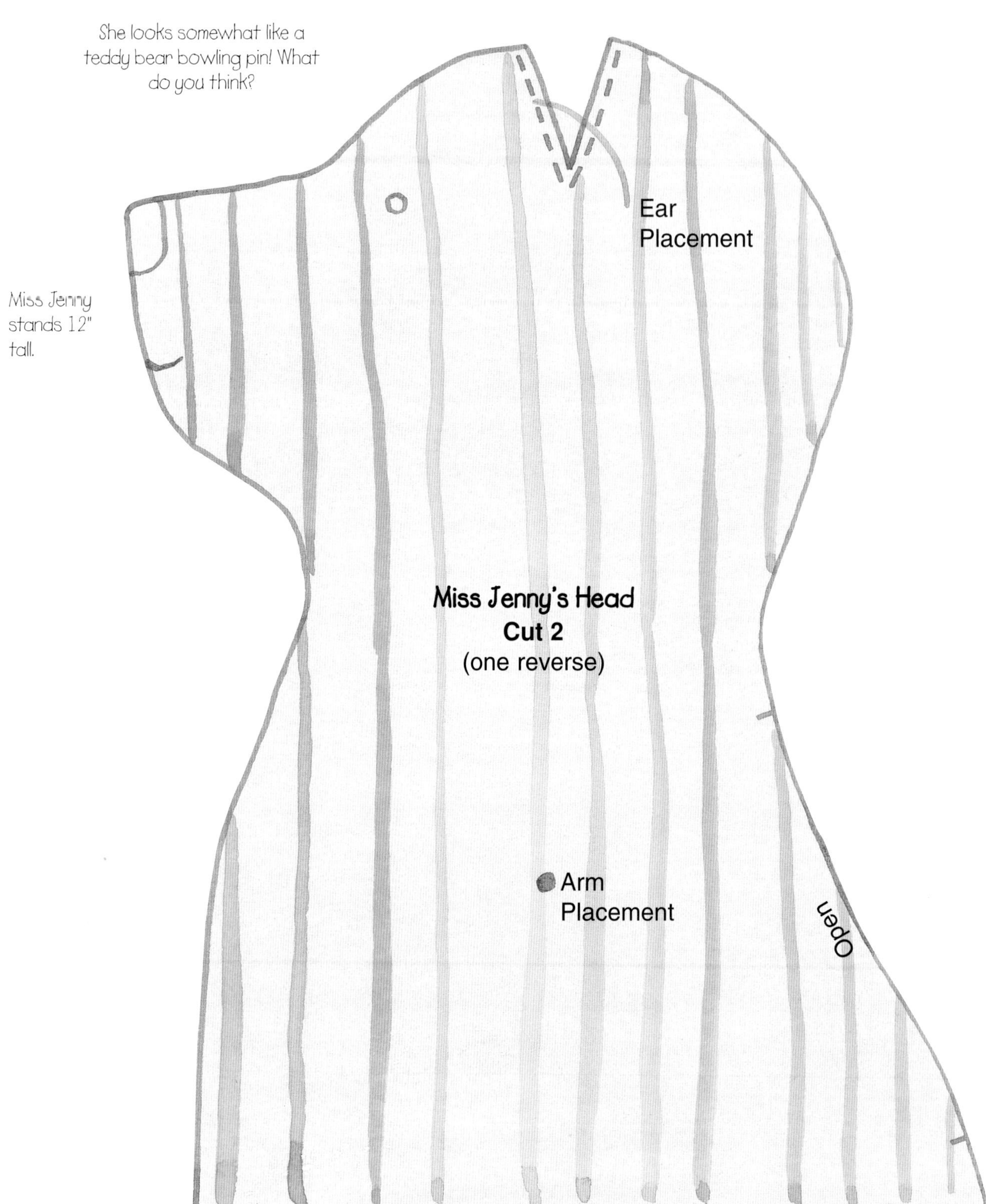

Attach pattern to bottom of pattern on page 102 with transparent tape before tracing and cutting fabric.

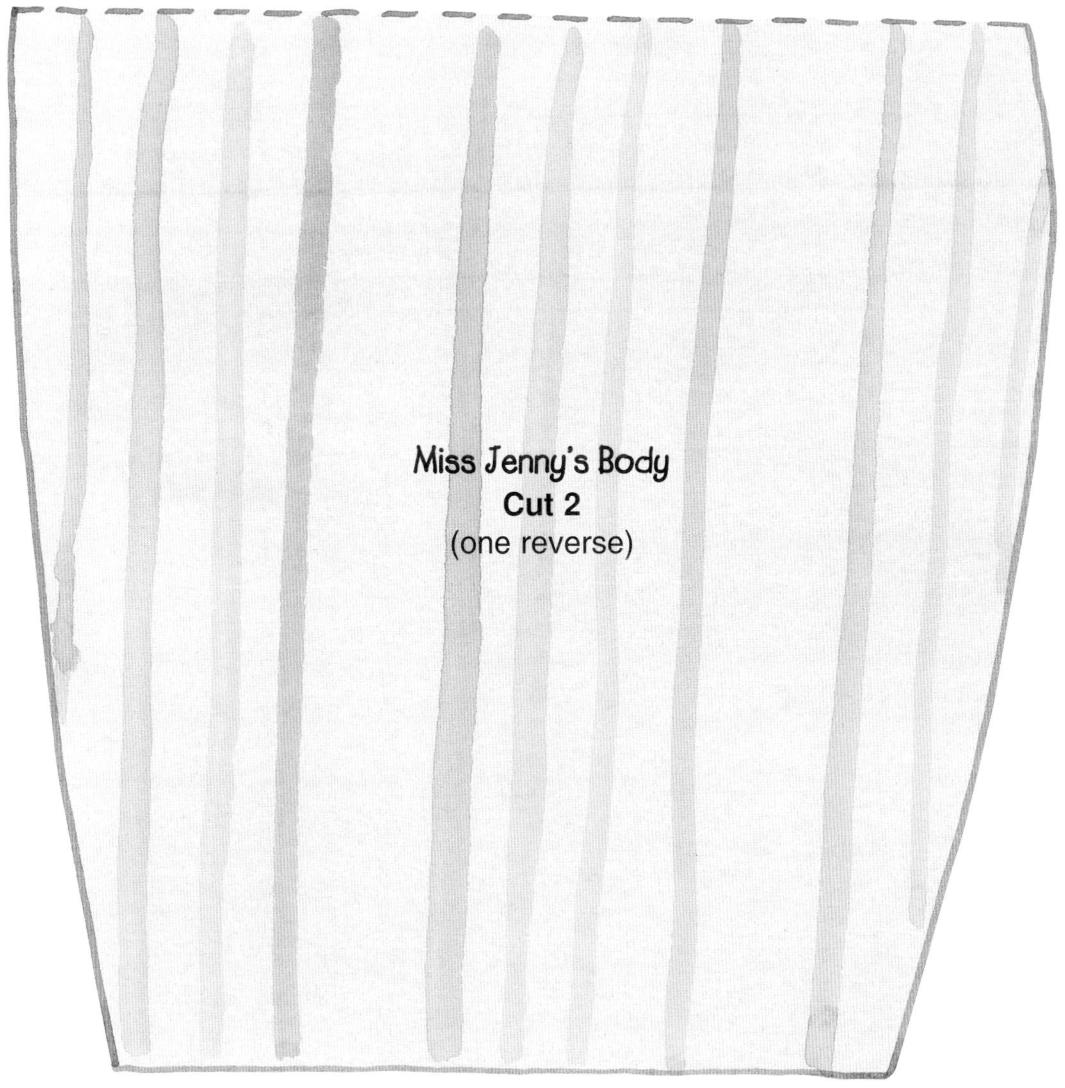

Continued from page 101.

Skirt

15. Using fabric scissors, cut two 8" x 24" pieces of fabric for skirt.

16. Using measuring tape, measure waist of bear. Using fabric scissors, cut $2^1/_2$"-wide band the length of waist measurement from fabric, creating waistband.

17. Using sewing machine, sew sides and bottom closed, with right sides together, leaving open at top. Turn right side out, creating skirt.

18. Fill bottom of skirt with plastic pellets and carefully sew top closed.

19. Gather-stitch two rows across top long edge of skirt to fit waistband.

20. Sew waistband onto skirt. The skirt will fit like an apron, open in the back.

21. Place skirt on bear. Using sewing needle, tack skirt on bear's waist with sewing thread.

Shawl

22. Using fabric scissors, cut 5" x 18" piece of loose-weave fabric for shawl.

23. Using sewing needle, pull threads out along all edges to create fringe.

24. Wrap shawl around shoulders.

25. Sew lace around neck. Pin shawl in place with brooch or sew on decorative button.

Broom

26. Break chop stick to desired length.

27. Using craft scissors, cut straw from kitchen broom and place around end of chop stick . Attach with twist tie.

28. Cover twist tie with ribbon. Adhere with glue.

Sash

29. Using fabric scissors, cut 22" x3" piece of fabric for sash.

30. Using sewing needle, pull threads out along all edges to create fringe.

31. Tie sash around bear's waist.

Hat (optional)

32. Trim straw hat with fabric bow. Adhere with glue.

33. Place hat on bear's head. Using sewing needle, tack to secure with sewing thread, or tuck in paw as shown below.

Miss Jenny, modeling her straw hat

Miss Jenny before adding clothing (Her weighted skirt and sash sit beside her.)

Miss Jenny sweeping as friend watches (Instructions for Miss Jenny's friend, see page 63. Reduce patterns as desired.)

Santa Bear

I collect Santa's and find them to be a wonderful keepsake of Christmases past. Any old blanket, shirt, coat, or plaid flannel will work to create this bear. Santa Bear's face has been dabbed with a cotton ball that was placed into strong coffee mixture.

Materials

Artificial beard: white
Artificial berries: sprig
Buttons: medium (2)
Embroidery floss: brown
Eyes: glass or safety, 8 mm, black
Fabrics: blanket or flannel (1/2 yd.) for body and coat; felt square (scrap) for nose; felt, synthetic fur, or quilt batting (1/4 yd.) for arms, ears, and head; mohair or synthetic fur (1/4 yd.) for trim
Plastic pellets: (1 cup)
Polyester stuffing: small bag
Ribbed sock: coordinating color of choice
Silk pine branches: small
Thread: heavy; sewing, coordinating color of choice

Tools

Cardboard
Fabric marker
Needles: doll, 5" or longer; embroidery; sewing
Pencil
Pins
Scissors: craft; fabric
Sewing machine with thread
Stuffing stick
Tracing paper

All seam allowances are 1/8".

Beginnings

1. Read "Bear Necessities" on pages 8-17 before beginning. Organize all materials and tools needed for this project.

2. Using pencil, tracing paper, cardboard, and craft scissors, make templates of pattern pieces on pages 109-112.

Continued on page 110.

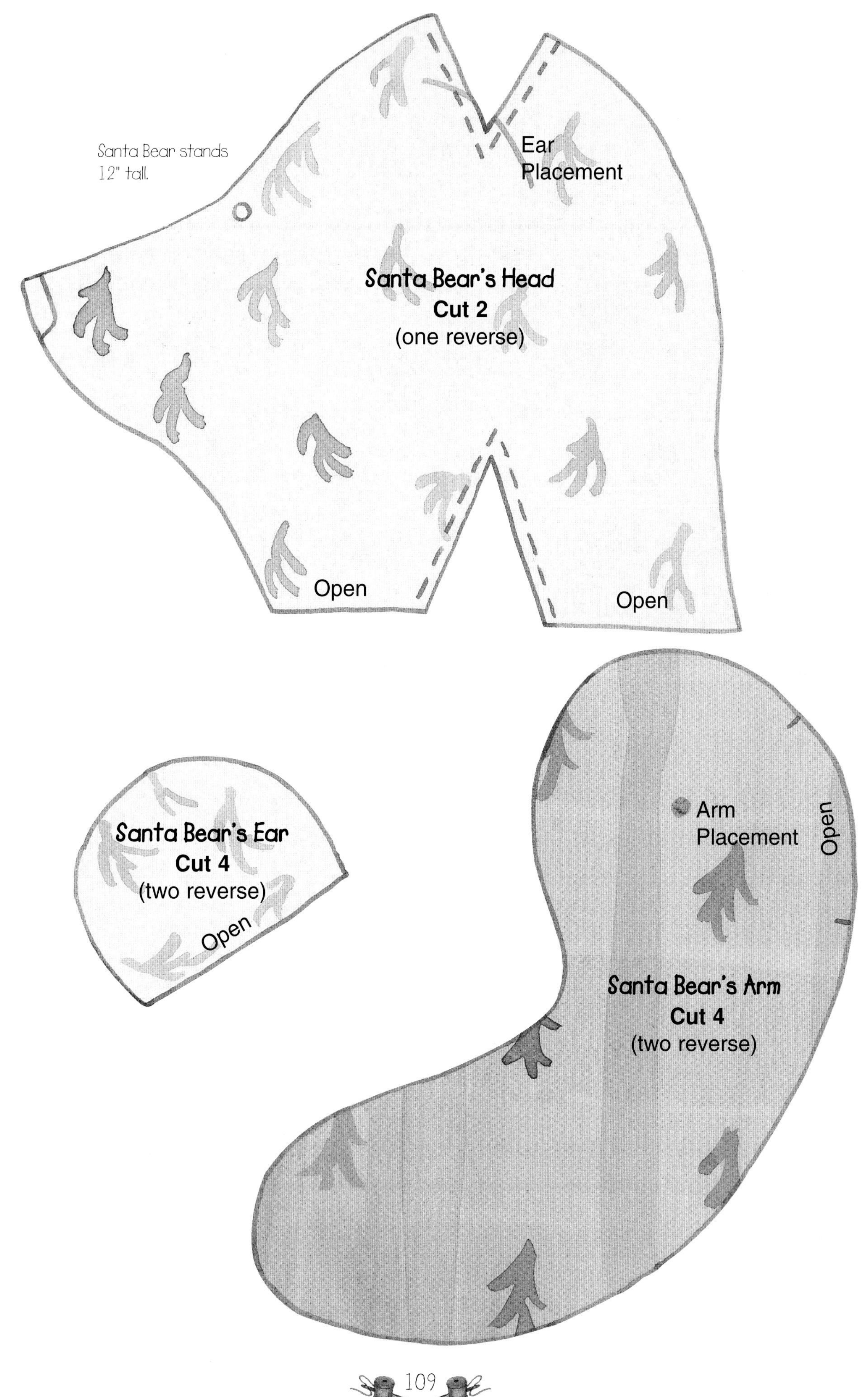
Santa Bear stands
12" tall.
Ear
Placement
Santa Bear's Head
Cut 2
(one reverse)
Open
Open
Santa Bear's Ear
Cut 4
(two reverse)
Open
Arm
Placement
Open
Santa Bear's Arm
Cut 4
(two reverse)

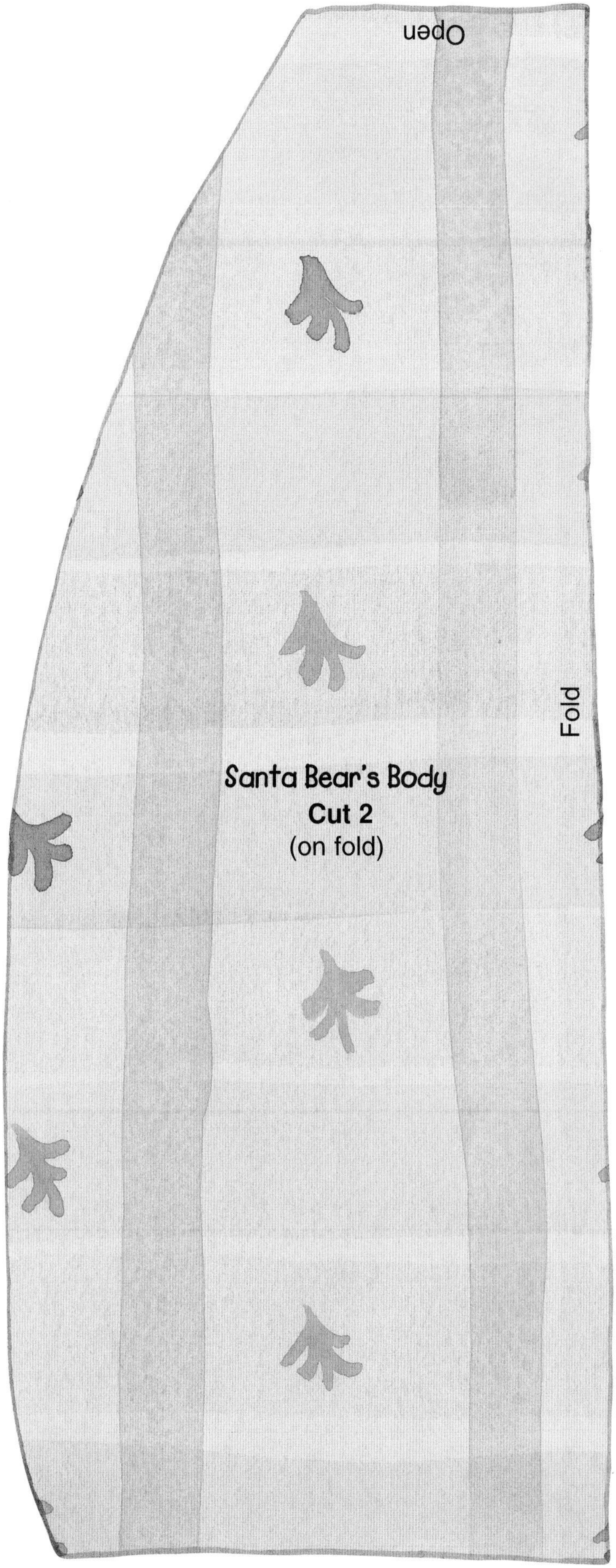

Open

Fold

Santa Bear's Body
Cut 2
(on fold)

Continued from page 108.

3. Place templates on backs of fabric. Using fabric marker, trace pattern. Using fabric scissors, cut out fabric pieces.

4. Using sewing machine, sew darts in head.

5. Sew head, ear, and arm pieces, with right sides together, leaving open where marked.

6. Sew body pieces, with right sides together, leaving open where marked. Square off bottom corners by folding bottom seam flat and sewing across corners. Check all seams. Turn all sewn pieces right side out.

Note: If using glass eyes, stuff head first. If using safety eyes, insert eyes and then stuff head.

7. Using stuffing stick, stuff head firmly with polyester stuffing. Stuff arms. Fill bottom of body with plastic pellets, then stuff body firmly to top with polyester stuffing.

8. See "Ladder Stitch" on page 15. Using embroidery needle, sew head and body closed with embroidery floss and Ladder Stitch.

Face

9. Using pins, mark eye placement. Using doll needle, pull eyes onto face with heavy thread.

10. Using pins, attach ears onto head where marked on pattern. See "Ladder Stitch" on page 15. Using embroidery needle, sew ears onto head with heavy thread and Ladder Stitch.

11. Using pencil, trace desired nose pattern from page 14 onto tracing paper, creating template. Using craft scissors, cut out template. Using fabric marker, trace template onto felt. Using fabric scissors, cut out felt nose. Pin felt nose onto face.

12. See "Satin Stitch" on page 15. Using embroidery needle, embroider over felt nose with embroidery floss and Satin Stitch. Embroider mouth.

Arms & Body

13. Using embroidery needle, gather-stitch around opening on body with heavy thread, leaving slightly open to fit base of head. Sew arms closed with heavy thread.

14. Using doll needle, sew arms onto body $2\frac{1}{2}$" from neck with heavy thread and buttons.

15. Align centers of head and body. See "Ladder Stitch" on page 15. Using Ladder Stitch, sew head onto body. Sew around neck twice for strength.

❤ See completed bear on page 113 before adding clothing.

Coat

All fur trim is turned fur up and hand hemmed for a more finished look.

16. Using sewing machine, sew dart in back of coat.

17. Sew shoulder seams, with right sides together, on coat. Gather-stitch sleeves. Ease sleeves into sleeve openings, pin, and sew.

18. Using fabric scissors, cut 2" strips from fabric for trim. Using sewing machine, sew to front edges, and wrist on sleeves.

19. Sew coat closed from wrist on sleeve to bottom of coat on each side.

20. Sew fur trim around bottom edge of coat.

Hat

21. Using fabric scissors, cut "hat" from old sock along dotted line. See Diagram A on page 112.

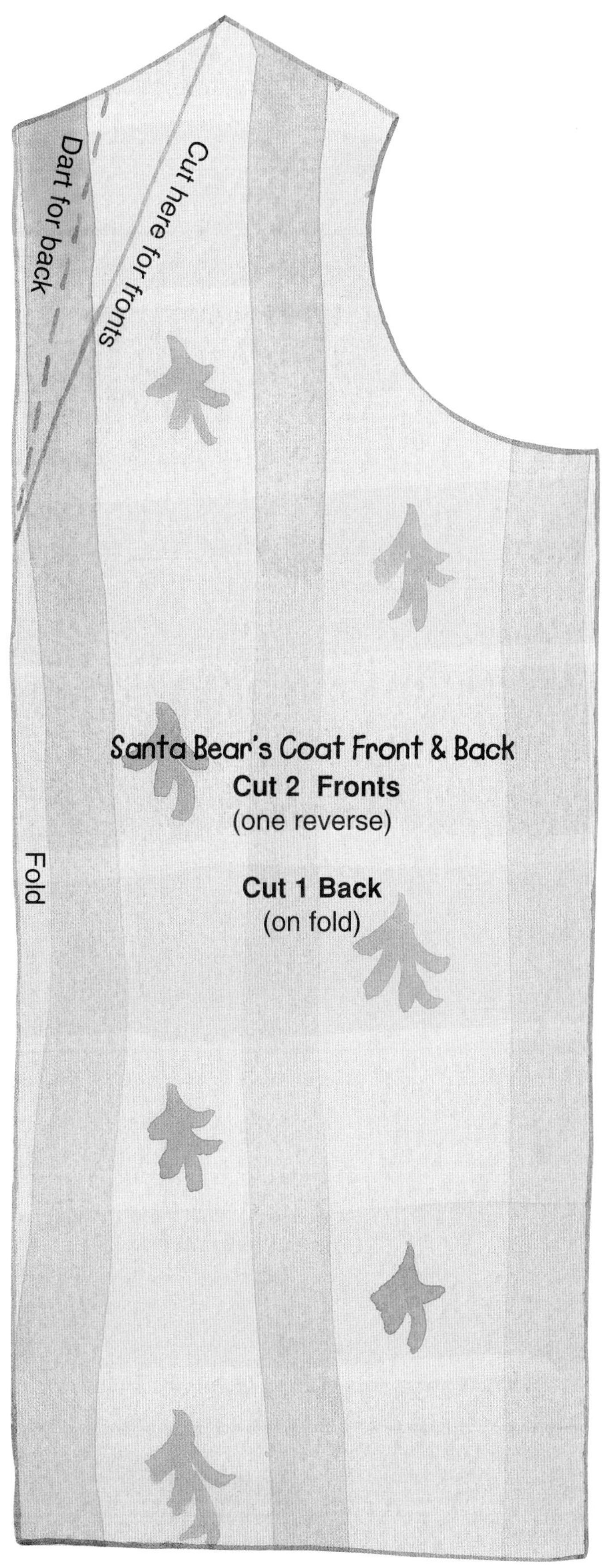

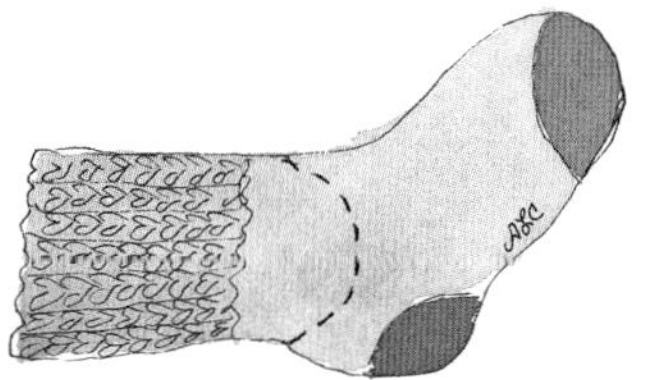

Diagram A

22. Using sewing needle, sew raw edges together with sewing thread, closing top of hat. Fold bottom edge up for brim.

23. Place hat on bear's head and tack to secure with sewing thread.

Beard

24. Using sewing needle, sew beard onto chin with sewing thread.

Finishings

25. Sew paws together with sewing thread.

26. Tuck berries and pine branches in paws and add berries to hat.

Add some festive shoes to Santa Bear. I found a pair of snow shoes for him to wear.

Santa Bear before adding clothing

Amy Rabbit is sewn similar to the Miss Gabby, who is on page 91. Amy Rabbit can sit in several different positions. She likes to carry a sewing basket full of sewing supplies or carrots.

Materials

Buttons: medium (2); small
Embroidery floss: brown, pink
Eyes: glass or safety, 8 mm, black
Fabrics: contrasting print ($^1/_4$ yd.) for apron and bib; felt square (scrap) for nose; felt square, black (scrap) for shoes; print ($^3/_4$ yd.) for body and legs, ($^1/_3$ yd.) for dress; synthetic fur or felt ($^1/_3$ yd.) for arms, ears, and head
Lace: $^1/_2$"-1"-wide (1 yd.); eyelet, 6"-wide (12")
Plastic pellets: (1 cup)
Plastic vegetable: small
Polyester stuffing: small bag
Thread: heavy; sewing, coordinating color of choice

Tools

Cardboard
Fabric marker
Needles: doll, 5" or longer; embroidery; sewing
Pencil
Pins
Scissors: craft; fabric
Sewing machine with thread
Stuffing stick
Tracing paper
Transparent tape

All seam allowances are $^1/_8$".

Beginnings

1. Read "Bear Necessities" on pages 8-17 before beginning. Organize all materials and tools needed for this project.

2. Using sewing machine, sew black felt onto bottom of leg fabric. See Diagram A on page 116.

3. Using pencil, tracing paper, cardboard, and craft scissors, make templates of pattern pieces on pages 116-119.

4. Place templates on backs of fabric. Using fabric marker, trace pattern. Trace leg pattern with shoe portion placed on black felt. Using fabric scissors,

cut out fabric pieces. Trace leg pattern with shoe portion placed on black felt. See Diagram A. Using fabric scissors, cut out fabric pieces.

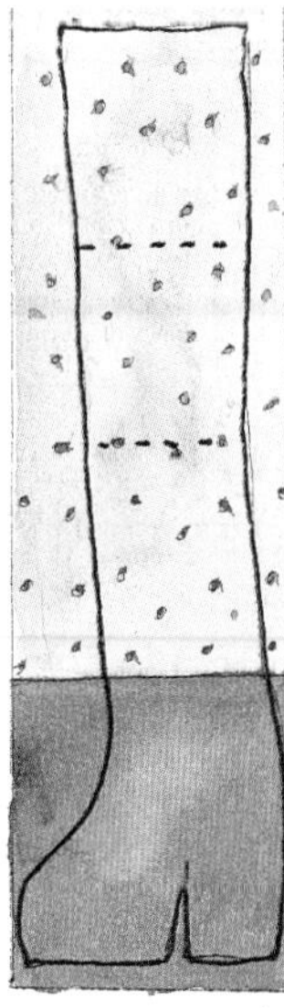

Diagram A

5. Using sewing machine, sew darts in head.

6. Sew head, ear, and arm pieces, with right sides together, leaving open where marked.

7. Sew body pieces, with center seams first. Sew sides and bottoms, with right sides together, leaving open where marked. Check all seams. Turn all sewn pieces right side out

Note: If using glass eyes, stuff head first. If using safety eyes, insert eyes first and then stuff head.

8. Using stuffing stick, stuff head firmly with polyester stuffing. Stuff arms. Fill bottom of body with plastic pellets, then stuff body firmly to the top with polyester stuffing.

Face

9. Using pins, mark eye placement. Using doll needle, pull eyes onto face with heavy thread.

10. Using pins, attach ears onto head where marked on pattern. See "Ladder Stitch" on page 15. Using Ladder Stitch, sew ears onto head. with heavy thread and Ladder Stitch.

11. Using pencil, trace desired nose pattern from

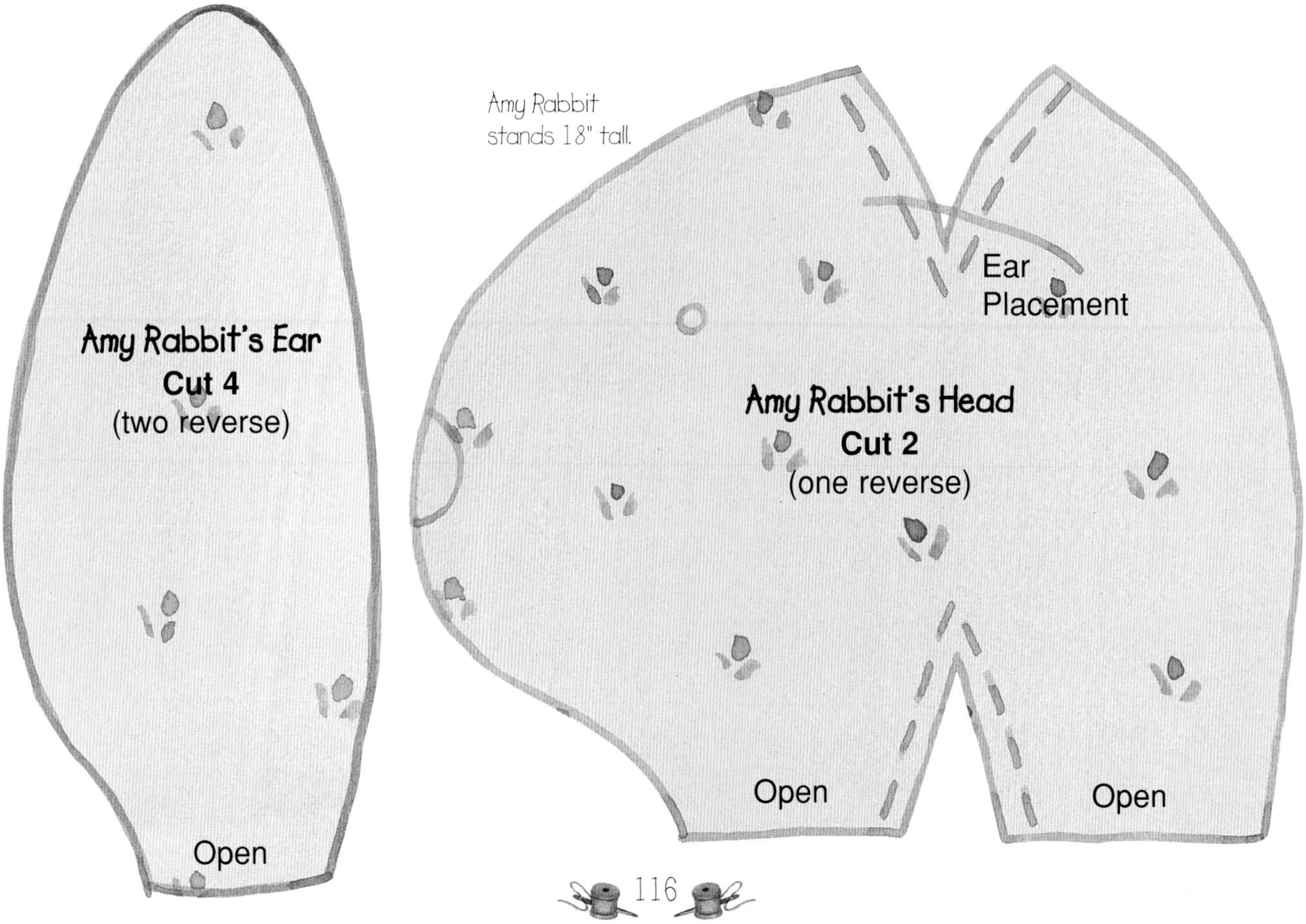

Amy Rabbit stands 18" tall.

Amy Rabbit's Ear
Cut 4
(two reverse)
Open

Amy Rabbit's Head
Cut 2
(one reverse)
Ear Placement
Open
Open

page 14 onto tracing paper, creating template. Using craft scissors, cut out template. Using fabric marker, trace template onto felt. Using fabric scissors, cut out felt nose. Pin felt nose onto face.

12. See "Satin Stitch" on page 15. Using embroidery needle, embroider over felt nose with embroidery floss and Satin Stitch. Embroider mouth.

Arms, Body, & Legs

13. Using embroidery needle, gather-stitch around opening on body with heavy thread, leaving slightly open to fit base of head. Sew arms closed.

14. Using doll needle, sew arms onto body with heavy thread and buttons.

15. Align center seams of head and body. See "Ladder Stitch" on page 15. Using Ladder Stitch, sew head onto body. Sew around neck twice for strength.

16. Using stuffing stick, stuff legs to first mark with polyester stuffing. Match seams. Using sewing machine, sew across legs. Feet will be facing forward.

17. Using stuffing stick, stuff legs 2" from top. Using sewing machine, sew across legs, leaving unstuffed section for hem.

18. Fold in hem to insides of legs. Using sewing machine, sew legs onto bottom of body. See diagram on page 94.

Shoes

19. Create shoe laces with embroidery floss.

Continued on page 120.

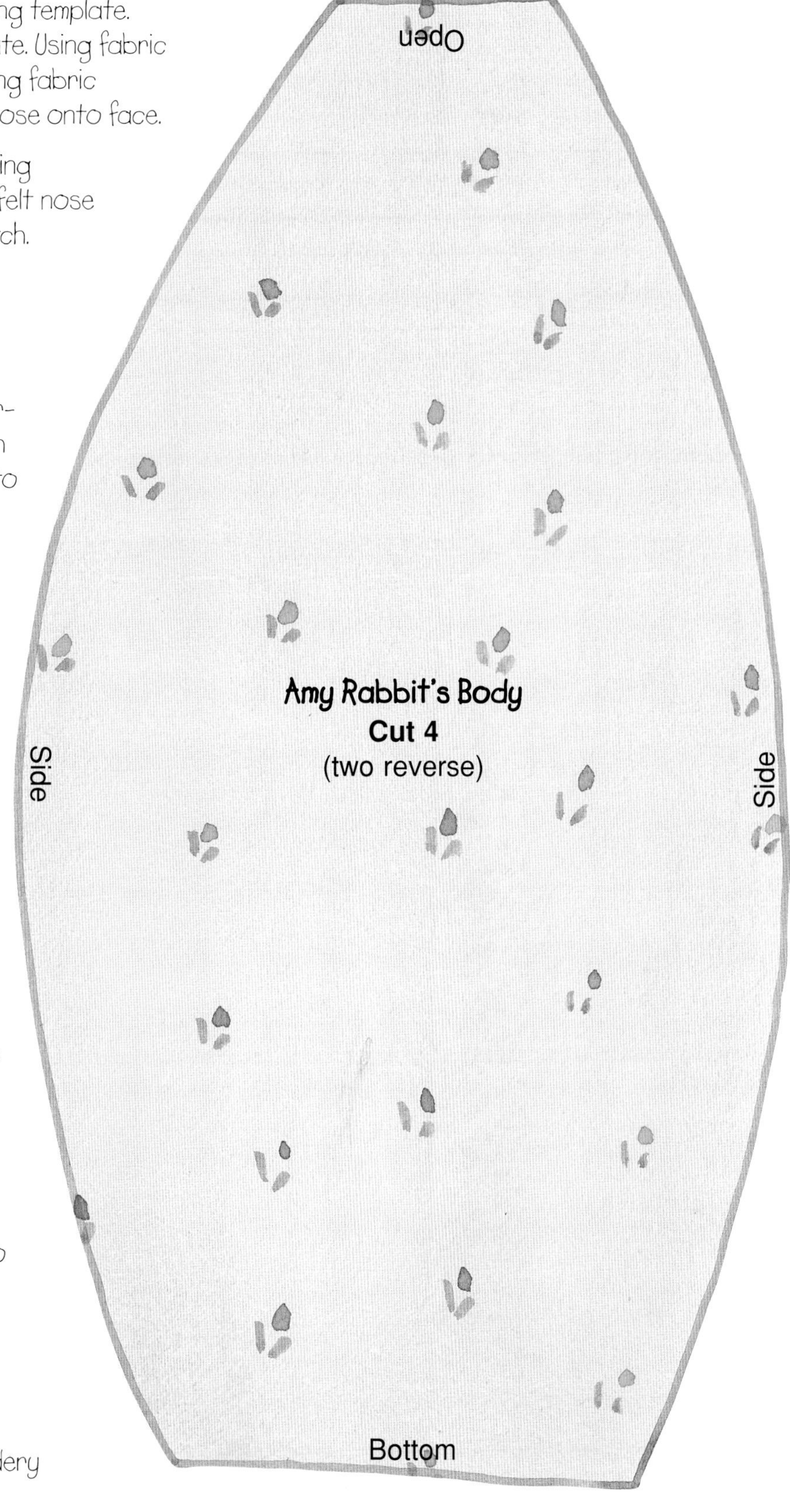

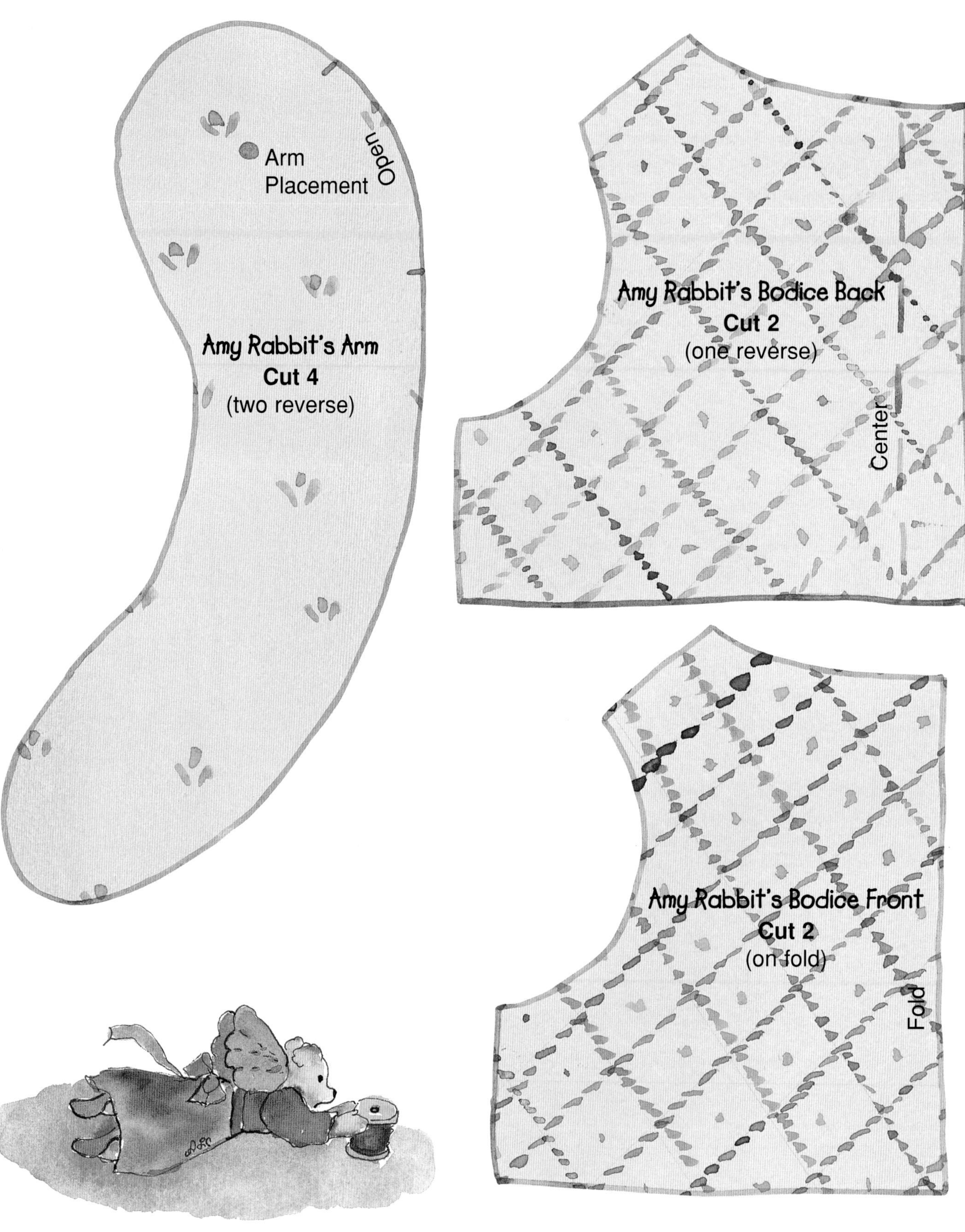
Arm
Placement
Open
Amy Rabbit's Arm
Cut 4
(two reverse)
Amy Rabbit's Bodice Back
Cut 2
(one reverse)
Center
Amy Rabbit's Bodice Front
Cut 2
(on fold)
Fold

Attach pattern piece to top of leg pattern with transparent tape.

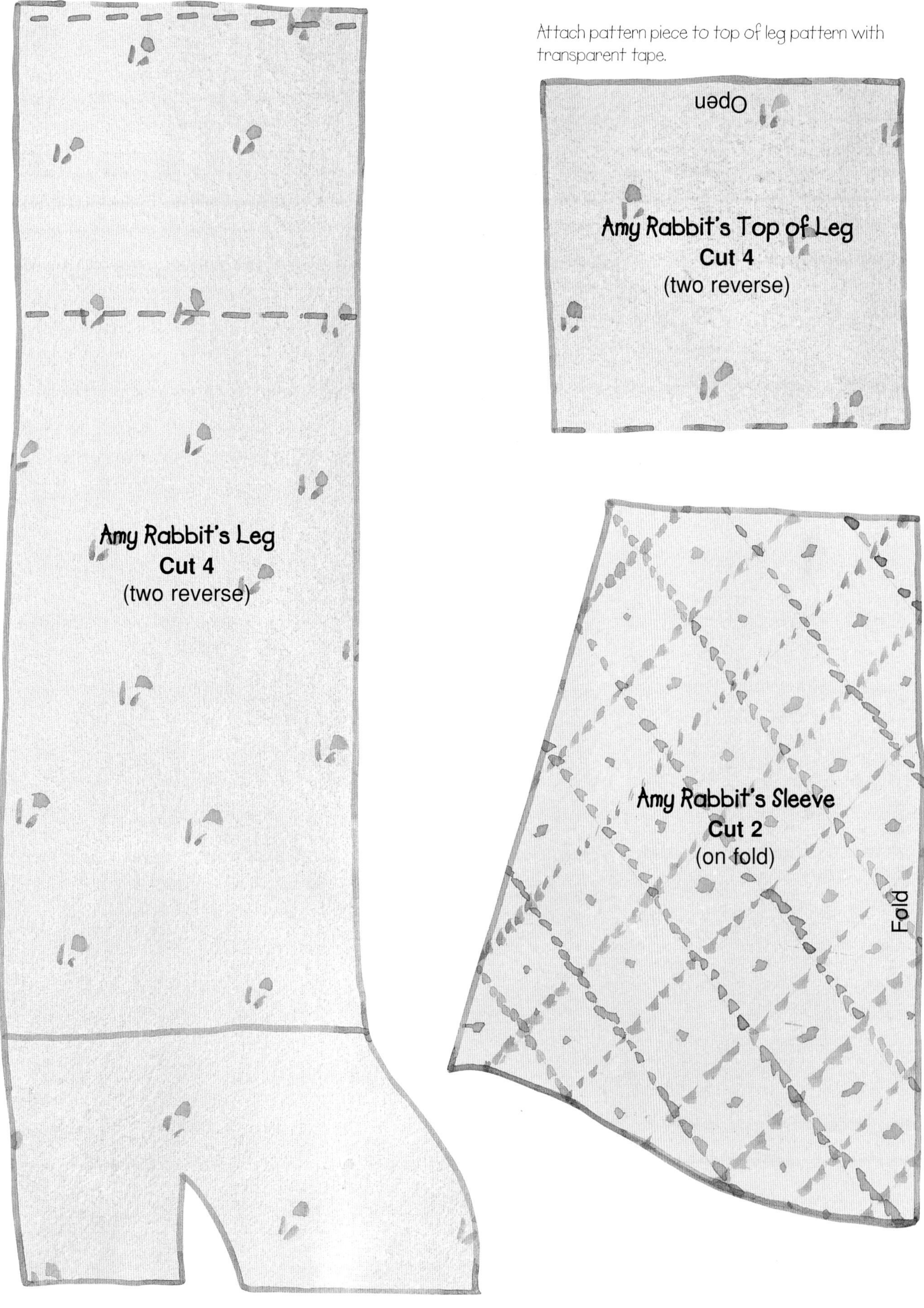

Continued from page 117.

Dress

20. Using fabric scissors, cut 12" x 33" piece of cotton for skirt.

21. Using sewing machine, gather-stitch top long edge of skirt.

22. Sew shoulder seams, with right sides together, on bodice. Turn down neck edge 1/4" and hem.

23. Gather-stitch top and bottom of sleeves, fitting sleeves to bear arms.

24. Sew lace trim at wrist on sleeves. Ease sleeves into sleeve openings, pin, and sew.

25. Sew bodice closed from wrist on sleeve to bottom of bodice on each side.

26. Sew gathered skirt to bodice.

27. Hem 2" on skirt bottom.

28. Sew up back seam to 1" from waist. Fold edge of opening in 1/4" and sew.

29. Sew lace trim onto neck edge.

30. Using sewing needle, sew snaps along edge of with sewing thread.

Apron & Bib

31. Using fabric scissors, cut two rectangles 6" x 12" and 3" x 4" of contrasting cotton for apron and bib. Cut two ties 3" x 8".

32. Using sewing machine, gather-stitch one 12" edge and sew to 4" edge of smaller rectangle.

33. Sew ties to sides.

34. Place around bunny's waist. Tie to secure.

35. Using sewing needle, tack two small buttons for trim to top of apron with sewing thread. See photo on page 114 for placement.

Finishings

36. Using sewing needle, sew bunny's paws together with sewing thread.

37. Place carrot in arms.

Amy Rabbit before attaching stuffed sections

Miss Daisey loves to spend time with her friends. Miss Daisey is sewn similar to Rachael, who is on page 30. However, her ears are much larger and placed closer together. She enjoys being in the kitchen or in the midst of your sewing materials.

Materials

Buttons: medium (2)
Embroidery floss: brown
Eyes: glass or safety, 8 mm, black
Fabrics: felt square (scrap) for nose; mohair or synthetic fur (¼ yd.) for arms, ears, and head; print (½ yd.) for body and dress
Plastic pellets: (1 cup)
Polyester stuffing: small bag
Ribbon: coordinating color of choice, width of choice (1 yd.)
Snaps: small (2)
Thread: heavy; sewing, coordinating color of choice

Tools

Cardboard
Fabric marker
Needles: doll, 5" or longer; embroidery; sewing
Pencil
Pins
Scissors: craft; fabric
Sewing machine with thread
Stuffing stick
Tracing paper

All seam allowances are ⅛".

Beginnings

1. Read "Bear Necessities" on pages 8–17 before beginning. Organize all materials and tools needed for this project.

2. Using pencil, tracing paper, cardboard, and craft scissors, make templates of pattern pieces on pages 123–125.

3. Place templates on backs of fabric. Using fabric marker, trace pattern. Using fabric scissors, cut out fabric pieces.

4. Using sewing machine, sew head, ear, and arm pieces, with right sides together, leaving open where marked.

5. Sew body pieces, with right sides together, leaving open where marked. Square off bottom corners by folding bottom seam flat and sewing across corners. Check all seams. Turn all sewn pieces right side out.

Note: If using glass eyes, stuff head first. If using safety eyes, insert eyes first and then stuff head.

6. Using stuffing stick, stuff head firmly with polyester stuffing. Stuff arms. Fill bottom of body with plastic pellets, then stuff body firmly to the top with polyester stuffing.

Face

7. Using pins, mark eye placement. Using doll needle, pull eyes onto face with heavy thread.

8. Using pins, attach ears onto head where marked on pattern. See "Ladder Stitch" on page 15. Using embroidery needle, sew ears onto head with heavy thread and Ladder Stitch.

9. Using pencil, trace desired nose pattern from page 14 onto tracing paper, creating template. Using craft scissors, cut out template. Using fabric marker, trace template onto felt. Using fabric scissors, cut out felt nose. Pin felt nose onto face.

Miss Daisey stands 9½" tall.

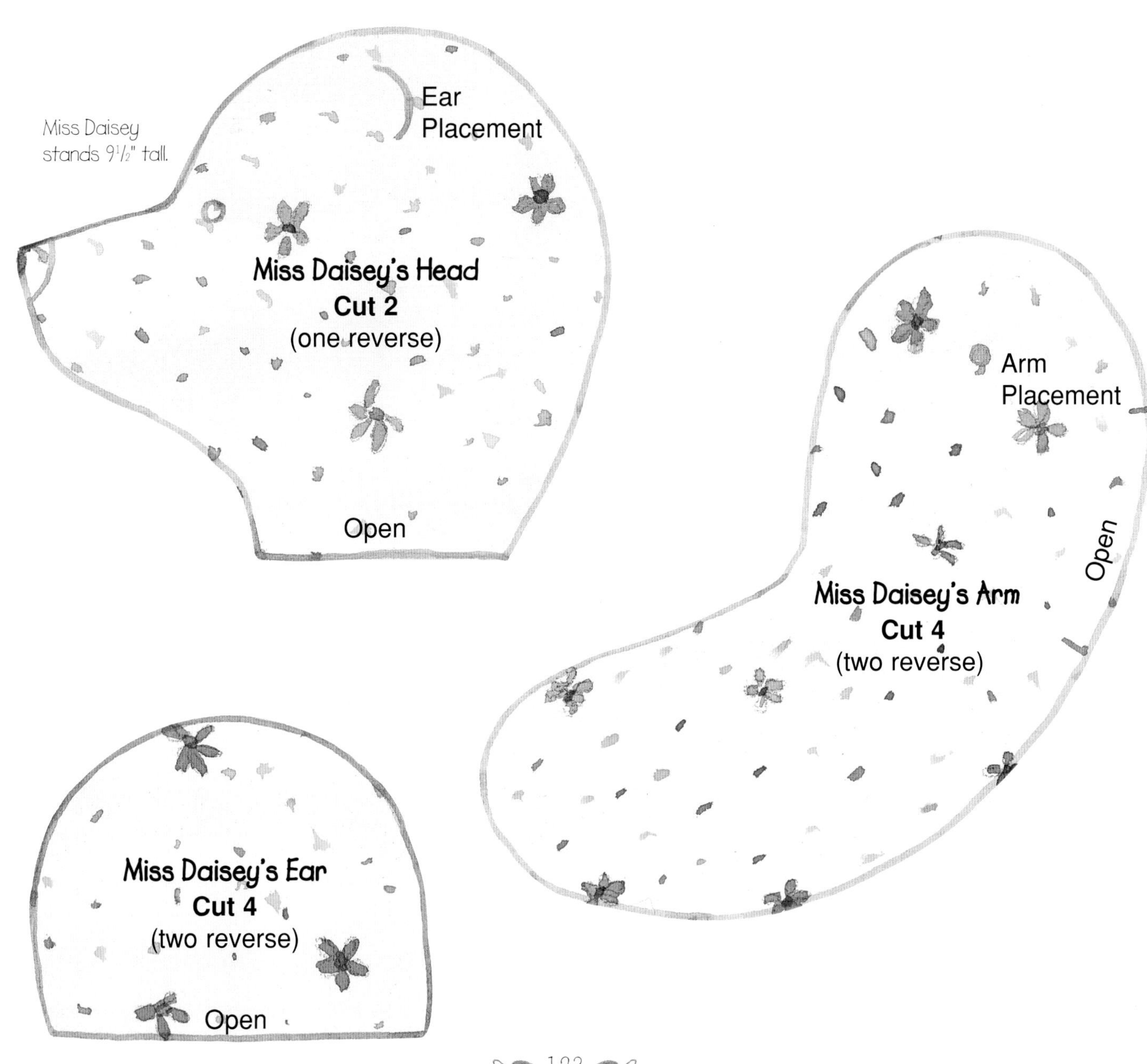

10. See "Satin Stitch" on page 15. Using embroidery needle, embroider over felt nose with embroidery floss and Satin Stitch. Embroider mouth.

Arms & Body

11. Using embroidery needle, gather-stitch around opening on body with heavy thread, leaving slightly open to fit base of head. Sew arms closed.

12. Using doll needle, sew arms onto body with heavy thread and buttons.

13. Align centers of head and body. See "Ladder Stitch" on page 15. Using embroidery needle, sew head onto body with heavy thread and Ladder Stitch. Sew around neck twice for strength.

Dress

14. Using fabric scissors, cut 8" x 19" piece of print fabric for skirt.

15. Using sewing machine, gather-stitch top long edge of skirt.

16. Sew shoulder seams, with right sides together, on dress. Turn down neck edge 1/8" and hem.

17. Turn up sleeve cuff and hem. Ease sleeves in sleeve openings. Sew under arms and side seams, creating bodice.

18. Sew gathered skirt to bodice.

19. Hem 2½" on skirt bottom.

20. Sew up back seam to 1" from waist. Fold edge of opening in and sew ¼".

21. Using sewing needle, sew snaps along edge with sewing thread.

Open

Arm Placement

Miss Daisey's Body
Cut 2
(on fold)

Fold

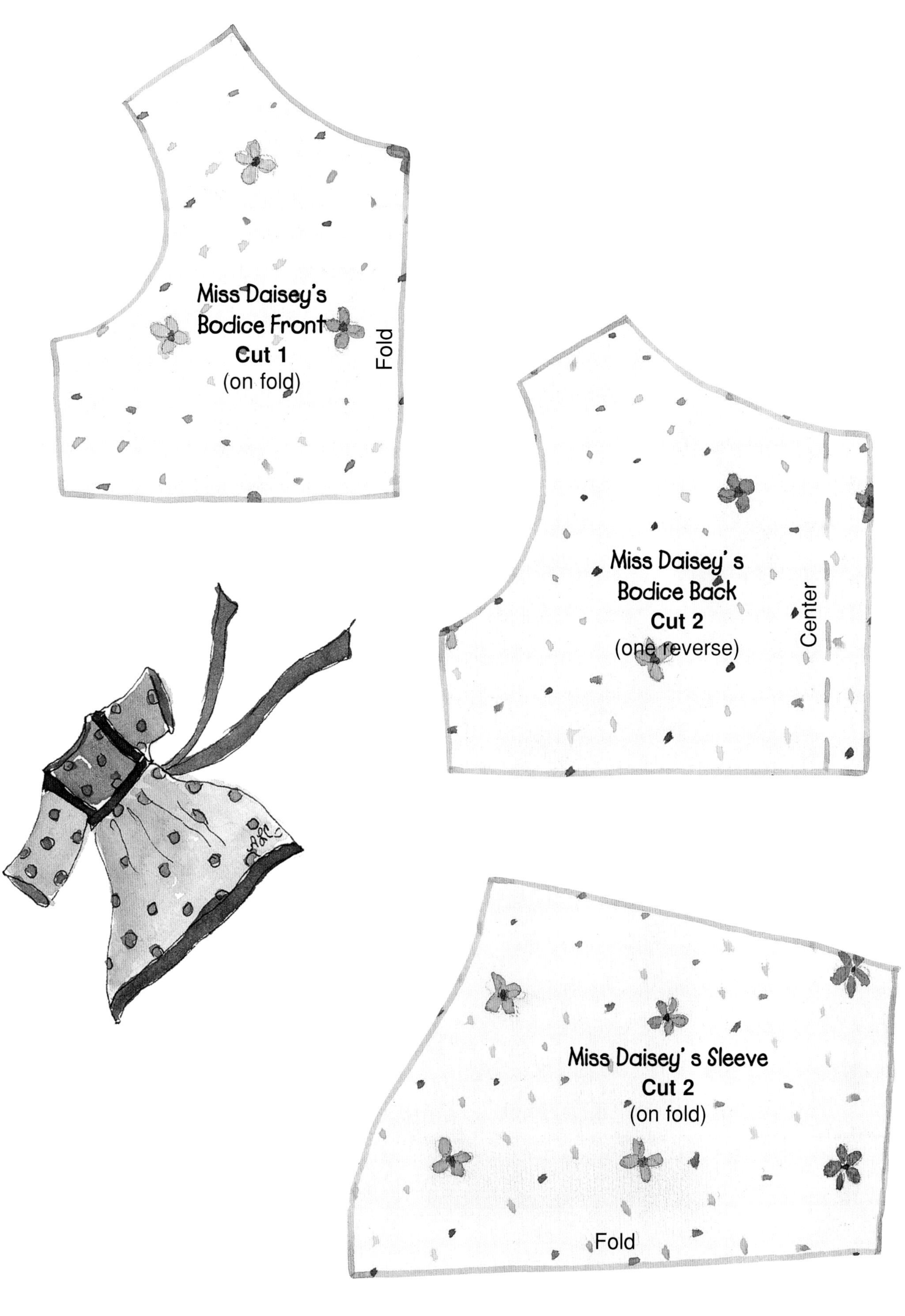
Miss Daisey's
Bodice Front
Cut 1
(on fold)
Fold
Miss Daisey' s
Bodice Back
Cut 2
(one reverse)
Center
Miss Daisey' s Sleeve
Cut 2
(on fold)
Fold

Miss Daisey and Colette, gathering sewing materials (Instructions for Colette, see page 47.)

Metric Conversion Chart

mm-millimetres cm-centimetres
inches to millimetres and centimetres

inches	mm	cm	inches	cm	inches	cm
1/8	3	0.3	9	22.9	30	76.2
1/4	6	0.6	10	25.4	31	78.7
1/2	13	1.3	12	30.5	33	83.8
5/8	16	1.6	13	33.0	34	86.4
3/4	19	1.9	14	35.6	35	88.9
7/8	22	2.2	15	38.1	36	91.4
1	25	2.5	16	40.6	37	94.0
1 1/4	32	3.2	17	43.2	38	96.5
1 1/2	38	3.8	18	45.7	39	99.1
1 3/4	44	4.4	19	48.3	40	101.6
2	51	5.1	20	50.8	41	104.1
2 1/2	64	6.4	21	53.3	42	106.7
3	76	7.6	22	55.9	43	109.2
3 1/2	89	8.9	23	58.4	44	111.8
4	102	10.2	24	61.0	45	114.3
4 1/2	114	11.4	25	63.5	46	116.8
5	127	12.7	26	66.0	47	119.4
6	152	15.2	27	68.6	48	121.9
7	178	17.8	28	71.1	49	124.5
8	203	20.3	29	73.7	50	127.0

yards to metres

yards	metres	yards	metres	yards	metres	yards	metres	yards	metres
1/8	0.11	2 1/8	1.94	4 1/8	3.77	6 1/8	5.60	8 1/8	7.43
1/4	0.23	2 1/4	2.06	4 1/4	3.89	6 1/4	5.72	8 1/4	7.54
3/8	0.34	2 3/8	2.17	4 3/8	4.00	6 3/8	5.83	8 3/8	7.66
1/2	0.46	2 1/2	2.29	4 1/2	4.11	6 1/2	5.94	8 1/2	7.77
5/8	0.57	2 5/8	2.40	4 5/8	4.23	6 5/8	6.06	8 5/8	7.89
3/4	0.69	2 3/4	2.51	4 3/4	4.34	6 3/4	6.17	8 3/4	8.00
7/8	0.80	2 7/8	2.63	4 7/8	4.46	6 7/8	6.29	8 7/8	8.12
1	0.91	3	2.74	5	4.57	7	6.40	9	8.23
1 1/8	1.03	3 1/8	2.86	5 1/8	4.69	7 1/8	6.52	9 1/8	8.34
1 1/4	1.14	3 1/4	2.97	5 1/4	4.80	7 1/4	6.63	9 1/4	8.46
1 3/8	1.26	3 3/8	3.09	5 3/8	4.91	7 3/8	6.74	9 3/8	8.57
1 1/2	1.37	3 1/2	3.20	5 1/2	5.03	7 1/2	6.86	9 1/2	8.69
1 5/8	1.49	3 5/8	3.31	5 5/8	5.14	7 5/8	6.97	9 5/8	8.80
1 3/4	1.60	3 3/4	3.43	5 3/4	5.26	7 3/4	7.09	9 3/4	8.92
1 7/8	1.71	3 7/8	3.54	5 7/8	5.37	7 7/8	7.20	9 7/8	9.03
2	1.83	4	3.66	6	5.49	8	7.32	10	9.14

Index